YORK NOTES

D1459415

GREAT EXPECTATIONS

CHARLES DICKENS

**NOTES BY DAVID LANGSTON AND MARTIN J. WALKER
REVISED BY LYN LOCKWOOD**

PEARSON

YORK PRESS

YORK PRESS
322 Old Brompton Road, London SW5 9JH

PEARSON EDUCATION LIMITED
Edinburgh Gate, Harlow,
Essex CM20 2JE, United Kingdom
Associated companies, branches and representatives throughout the world

First published 1997
New editions 2002 and 2015
This new and fully revised edition 2016

10 9 8 7 6

ISBN 978–1–4479–8215–9

Illustrations by Fausto Bianchi and Alan Batley (page 70 only)
Phototypeset by Carnegie Book Production
Printed in Malaysia, CTP-PJB

Photo credits: Bogdan Ionescu/Shutterstock for page 8 top / © iStock/vasiliki for page 9
top / © iStock/Gordonsaunders for page 12 bottom / Ppictures/Shutterstock for page 15
bottom / Africa Studio/Shutterstock for page 17 bottom / Alexander Tihonov/
Shutterstock for page 18 bottom / Damon Yancy/Shutterstock for page 19 bottom /
Charlie Edward/Shutterstock for page 20 bottom / studioVin/Shutterstock for page 22
middle / Tosoth/Shutterstock for page 23 middle / Thomas Brain/Shutterstock for page
24 bottom / Madlen/Shutterstock for page 25 top / Anneka/Shutterstock for page 26
bottom / Anneka/Shutterstock for page 27 bottom / CreativeNature R. Zwerver/
Shutterstock for page 29 bottom / Marcin Neimiec/Shutterstock for page 30 bottom /
Paulrommer/Shutterstock for page 31 middle / Valentina Proskurina/Shutterstock for
page 33 bottom / Roman Samokhin/Shutterstock for page 35 middle / Everett
Historical/Shutterstock for page 37 bottom / Andreiuc88/Shutterstock for page 38
bottom / Unverdorben JR/Shutterstock for page 41 bottom / David Hughes/
Shutterstock for page 43 bottom / Schankz/Shutterstock for page 44 middle / Dennis
Albert Richardson/Shutterstock for page 45 middle / konstantin32/Thinkstock for page
51 bottom / Lassedesignen/Shutterstock for page 53 bottom / Det-anan/Shutterstock
for page 59 top / Catalin Eremia/Shutterstock for page 60 middle / Gary Yim/
Shutterstock for page 62 top / Siberia – Video and Photo/Shutterstock for page 65
bottom / Kunertus/Shutterstock for page 67 bottom / pgaborphotos/Shutterstock for
page 73 middle / Gordon J.A. Dixon/Shutterstock for page 74 bottom / Volodymyr
Tysba/Shutterstock for page 76 top / vavuzunlu/Shutterstock for page 78 bottom /
Wavebreakmedia/ Shutterstock for page 87 middle

CONTENTS

PREPARING FOR ASSESSMENT

HOW WILL I BE ASSESSED ON MY WORK ON *GREAT EXPECTATIONS?*

All exam boards are different but whichever course you are following, your work will be examined through these four Assessment Objectives:

Assessment Objectives	Wording	Worth thinking about ...
AO1	Read, understand and respond to texts. Students should be able to: • maintain a critical style and develop an informed personal response • use textual references, including quotations, to support and illustrate interpretations.	• How well do I know what happens, what people say, do, etc? • What do *I* think about the key ideas in the novel? • How can I support my viewpoint in a really convincing way? • What are the best quotations to use and when should I use them?
AO2	Analyse the language, form and structure used by a writer to create meanings and effects, using relevant subject terminology where appropriate.	• What specific things does the writer 'do'? What choices has Dickens made? (Why this particular word, phrase or paragraph here? Why does this event happen at this point?) • What effects do these choices create? Suspense? Ironic laughter? Reflective mood?
AO3	Show understanding of the relationships between texts and the contexts in which they were written.	• What can I learn about society from the novel? (What does it tell me about wealth and inheritance in Dickens's day, for example?) • What was society like in Dickens's time? Can I see it reflected in the story?
AO4*	Use a range of vocabulary and sentence structures for clarity, purpose and effect, with accurate spelling and punctuation.	• How accurately and clearly do I write? • Are there small errors of grammar, spelling and punctuation that I can get rid of?

*AO4 is assessed by OCR only

Look out for the Assessment Objective labels throughout your York Notes Study Guide – these will help to focus your study and revision!

The text used in this Study Guide is the Heinemann edition, 1993.

HOW TO USE YOUR YORK NOTES STUDY GUIDE

You are probably wondering what is the best and most efficient way to use your York Notes Study Guide on *Great Expectations*. Here are three possibilities:

A **step-by-step** study and revision guide	A **'dip-in' support** when you need it	A **revision guide** after you have finished the novel
Step 1: Read Part Two as you read the novel, as a companion to help you study it. **Step 2:** When you need to, turn to Parts Three to Five to focus your learning. **Step 3:** Then, when you have finished, use Parts Six and Seven to hone your exam skills, revise and practise for the exam.	Perhaps you know the book quite well, but you want to check your understanding and practise your exam skills? Just look for the section you think you need most help with and go for it!	You might want to use the Notes after you have finished your study, using Parts Two to Five to check over what you have learned, and then work through Parts Six and Seven in the immediate weeks leading up to your exam.

HOW WILL THE GUIDE HELP YOU STUDY AND REVISE?

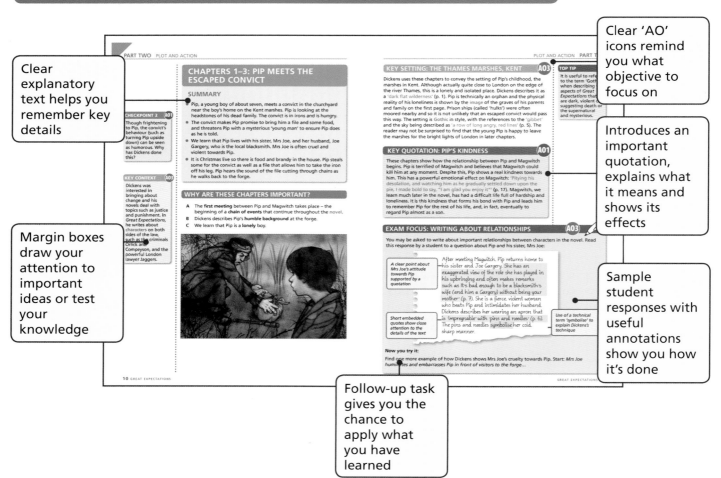

Clear explanatory text helps you remember key details

Margin boxes draw your attention to important ideas or test your knowledge

Clear 'AO' icons remind you what objective to focus on

Introduces an important quotation, explains what it means and shows its effects

Sample student responses with useful annotations show you how it's done

Follow-up task gives you the chance to apply what you have learned

Extra references to help you focus your revision

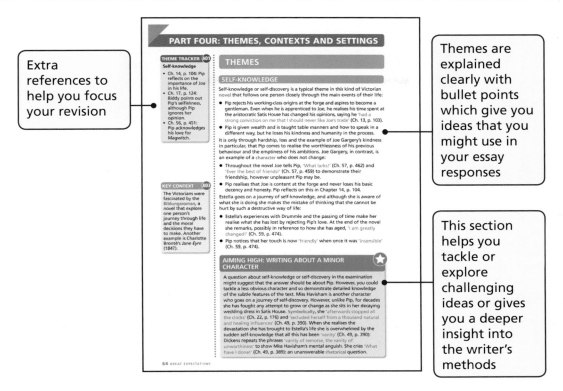

Themes are explained clearly with bullet points which give you ideas that you might use in your essay responses

This section helps you tackle or explore challenging ideas or gives you a deeper insight into the writer's methods

Parts Two to Five end with a **Progress and Revision Check**:

A set of quick questions tests your knowledge of the text

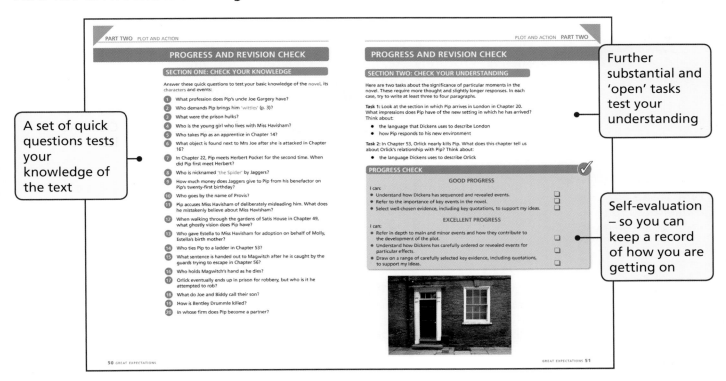

Further substantial and 'open' tasks test your understanding

Self-evaluation – so you can keep a record of how you are getting on

Don't forget Parts Six and Seven, with advice and practice on **improving your writing skills**:

- Focus on **difficult areas** such as **'context'** and **'inferences'**
- **Short snippets** of **other students' work** to show you how it's done (or not done!)
- Three annotated **sample responses** to a task **at different levels**, with **expert comments**, to help you judge your own level
- **Practice questions**
- **Answers** to the **Progress and Revision Checks** and **Checkpoint** margin boxes

Now it's up to you! Don't forget – there's even more help on our website with more sample answers, essay planners and even online tutorials. Go to www.yorknotes.com to find out more.

PLOT SUMMARY: WHAT HAPPENS IN *GREAT EXPECTATIONS*?

CHAPTERS 1–11: PIP'S CHILDHOOD

CHECKPOINT 1 **A02**

Why is Pip in the churchyard?

Pip, a young boy of about seven, meets a convict in the churchyard near his home on the Kent marshes, near London. We later find out that this convict is Magwitch. Pip lives with his sister, Mrs Joe, and her husband, Joe Gargery, who is the local blacksmith. The convict makes Pip bring him a file, to cut the irons off his leg, and some food. Pip steals the items and takes them to the convict who then disappears. As the food is missed from the house, soldiers looking for two escaped convicts arrive and seek the help of Joe to make new chains and leg irons. Pip does not betray the convict but he is found by the soldiers on the marshes, fighting with another escaped prisoner (who we later learn is called Compeyson). Magwitch is so determined not to let the other prisoner go that both men end up being caught.

Some time later Pip is invited to play at the large and intimidating Satis House with its strange inhabitant, Miss Havisham. She spends her days dressed in a faded wedding dress, surrounded by decaying wedding items such as a rotting cake, having been jilted at the altar. The rooms she occupies have not seen daylight for many years and neither has she. She has an adopted daughter, Estella, who is about Pip's age. Miss Havisham makes Pip play cards with Estella. Estella delights in humiliating him, but he finds her beautiful anyway and his love for her grows even as he becomes an adult.

CHECKPOINT 2 **A02**

Who is the boy who challenges Pip to a fight at Satis House?

A strange visitor to town gives Pip two pound notes and the man clearly has some connection with Pip's convict because he stirs his drink with the file that Pip stole. Pip meets the Pockets at Miss Havisham's and a strange boy makes Pip fight with him (later named as Herbert).

CHAPTERS 12–19: PIP'S EDUCATION AND APPRENTICESHIP

Miss Havisham pays Joe to take Pip on as his apprentice and he is sworn to the trade of blacksmith. Pip is not satisfied with his position in life and feels that he should be destined for greater things than being a blacksmith. To better himself, Pip attends a poorly run night class in the town where he meets Biddy, a bright girl of a similar age to himself. Mrs Joe is attacked and injured so severely that she can no longer speak. Pip suspects Orlick, Joe's assistant, who argued with his sister earlier the same day.

A stranger arrives from London and announces himself as Mr Jaggers, a lawyer. Pip has seen him before at Satis House. He tells Pip that he will inherit a large property and that he must go to London immediately to begin his training in life as a gentleman. As a condition, Pip is not to seek to discover who his mysterious benefactor is, though he assumes that it is Miss Havisham. Pip goes to London, leaving Joe and Biddy behind.

CHAPTERS 20–35: PIP MOVES TO LONDON

In London, Pip begins his education with Matthew Pocket, Miss Havisham's cousin, and becomes friends with his son Herbert. Jaggers is a cautious and clever lawyer who is always on his guard and Pip becomes friendly with his clerk, Wemmick. Pip gets into debt, but arranges for Herbert to be helped in his career. Pip is asked to accompany Estella in London. This strengthens his belief that Miss Havisham is paying for him to be educated as a gentleman so that he will be suitable to marry Estella. Estella tries to warn him that she has no feelings for him. Mrs Joe eventually dies from the injuries inflicted by Orlick, and Pip attends her funeral. Joe's subsequent visit to Pip in London is an embarrassing occasion for them both.

CHAPTERS 36–42: THE RETURN OF MAGWITCH

One night Pip has a surprise visitor: the convict from the beginning of the novel, Abel Magwitch. He is Pip's secret benefactor and has returned illegally from Australia to see Pip. Pip is shocked, because this destroys his dream that he and Estella will marry; and he is unnerved by the convict, but feels he should shelter him. Pip decides to get Magwitch out of the country. Pip learns that the convict Magwitch fought with on the marshes, and whom Magwitch blames for most of his troubles, is called Compeyson. This is the man who tricked Miss Havisham and failed to turn up to marry her.

> **TOP TIP** (A02)
>
> All of the mysteries from the first two thirds of the book are resolved in the final part. Look at the way that Dickens keeps the reader waiting.

CHAPTERS 43–55: ESTELLA MARRIES, PIP AND MAGWITCH GROW CLOSER

Pip learns that Estella will marry a brutal man called Bentley Drummle. Wemmick warns Pip that he and Magwitch are being watched. They hope to help Magwitch catch a foreign steamer and escape. Gradually Pip pieces together the information that Magwitch is Estella's father and that Jaggers's housekeeper, Molly, is her mother. Estella was placed in the care of Miss Havisham who adopted her.

CHAPTERS 56–9: THE DEATH OF MISS HAVISHAM, PIP AND ESTELLA RE-UNITED

After regretting her past mistakes and helping Pip to finance Herbert in business, Miss Havisham is injured when her wedding dress accidentally catches fire; she later dies from her injuries and Pip is badly burnt. Orlick plans to murder Pip having confessed to attacking Mrs Joe, but Herbert Pocket comes to the rescue. As Pip and Magwitch attempt to catch the ship, they are caught by the police. In the struggle, Compeyson is drowned. Magwitch is sentenced to death for returning to England but dies in prison. Pip tells him that his daughter is a beautiful lady and that he, Pip, loves her.

Pip falls ill and is nursed by Joe. When he is well, he decides to go home and ask Biddy to marry him. He arrives to find she is marrying Joe. Pip accepts Herbert's offer of a job with his firm in Cairo. He returns after eleven years and accidentally meets Estella in the grounds of Satis House. She is now a widow. Pip feels sure that he and Estella will never part again.

CHAPTERS 1–3: PIP MEETS THE ESCAPED CONVICT

SUMMARY

- Pip, a young boy of about seven, meets a convict in the churchyard near the boy's home on the Kent marshes. Pip is looking at the headstones of his dead family. The convict is in irons and is hungry.
- The convict makes Pip promise to bring him a file and some food, and threatens Pip with a mysterious 'young man' to ensure Pip does as he is told.
- We learn that Pip lives with his sister, Mrs Joe, and her husband, Joe Gargery, who is the local blacksmith. Mrs Joe is often cruel and violent towards Pip.
- It is Christmas Eve so there is plenty of food and brandy in the house. Pip steals some for the convict as well as a file that allows him to take the iron off his leg. Pip hears the sound of the file cutting through chains as he walks back to the forge.

WHY ARE THESE CHAPTERS IMPORTANT?

A The **first meeting** between Pip and Magwitch takes place – the beginning of a **chain of events** that continue throughout the **novel**.

B Dickens describes Pip's **humble background** at the forge.

C We learn that Pip is a **lonely** boy.

CHECKPOINT 3

Though frightening to Pip, the convict's behaviour (such as turning Pip upside down) can be seen as humorous. Why has Dickens done this?

KEY CONTEXT A03

Dickens was interested in bringing about change and his novels deal with topics such as justice and punishment. In *Great Expectations*, he writes about **characters** on both sides of the law, such as the criminals Orlick and Compeyson, and the powerful London lawyer Jaggers.

KEY SETTING: THE THAMES MARSHES, KENT A03

Dickens uses these chapters to convey the setting of Pip's childhood, the marshes in Kent. Although actually quite close to London on the edge of the river Thames, this is a lonely and isolated place. Dickens describes it as a 'dark flat wilderness' (p. 1). Pip is technically an orphan and the physical reality of his loneliness is shown by the **image** of the graves of his parents and family on the first page. Prison ships (called 'hulks') were often moored nearby and so it is not unlikely that an escaped convict would pass this way. The setting is **Gothic** in style, with the references to the 'gibbet' and the sky being described as 'a row of long angry, red lines' (p. 5). The reader may not be surprised to find that the young Pip is happy to leave the marshes for the bright lights of London in later chapters.

TOP TIP A01

It is useful to refer to the term 'Gothic' when describing the aspects of *Great Expectations* that are dark, violent or suggesting death or the supernatural and mysterious.

KEY QUOTATION: PIP'S KINDNESS A01

These chapters show how the relationship between Pip and Magwitch begins. Pip is terrified of Magwitch and believes that Magwitch could kill him at any moment. Despite this, Pip shows a real kindness towards him. This has a powerful emotional effect on Magwitch: 'Pitying his desolation, and watching him as he gradually settled down upon the pie, I made bold to say, "I am glad you enjoy it"' (p. 17). Magwitch, we learn much later in the novel, has had a difficult life full of hardship and loneliness. It is this kindness that forms his bond with Pip and leads him to remember Pip for the rest of his life, and, in fact, eventually to regard Pip almost as a son.

EXAM FOCUS: WRITING ABOUT RELATIONSHIPS A03

You may be asked to write about important relationships between characters in the novel. Read this response by a student to a question about Pip and his sister, Mrs Joe:

A clear point about Mrs Joe's attitude towards Pip supported by a quotation

After meeting Magwitch, Pip returns home to his sister and Joe Gargery. She has an exaggerated view of the role she has played in his upbringing and often makes remarks such as 'It's bad enough to be a blacksmith's wife (and him a Gargery) without being your mother' (p. 7). She is a fierce, violent woman who beats Pip and intimidates her husband. Dickens describes her wearing an apron that is 'impregnable' with 'pins and needles' (p. 6). The pins and needles symbolise her cold, sharp manner.

Short, embedded quotes show close attention to the details of the text

*Use of a technical term, **symbolise** to explain Dickens's technique*

Now you try it:

Find one more example of how Dickens shows Mrs Joe's cruelty towards Pip. Start: *Mrs Joe humiliates and embarrasses Pip in front of visitors to the forge…*

CHAPTERS 4–6: THE HUNT FOR THE CONVICT

SUMMARY

- Pip says that he has been to hear the Christmas carols to explain why he left the house that morning, to cover up the fact that he has been to see the convict.
- Joe and Pip go to church after which visitors arrive for dinner: Mr Wopsle, the clerk at the church, Mr and Mrs Hubble and Mr Pumblechook, Joe's uncle.
- At the end of the meal, Mrs Joe offers Pumblechook some brandy. Pip is terrified as he took some of the brandy to the convict and has unwisely topped it up with strong-tasting tar-water.
- The sergeant interrupts as Pumblechook is coughing and choking. For a moment the terrified Pip thinks the sergeant's handcuffs are for him, but they just need repair.
- The soldiers, Pip and Joe hunt down the convicts and discover Magwitch and Compeyson fighting desperately in a ditch. Magwitch saves Pip from trouble when he says that he stole the food from the blacksmith's house.

WHY ARE THESE CHAPTERS IMPORTANT?

A We learn that Pip has a **strong sense of right and wrong** and is troubled by not being able to own up to Joe about stealing the food. He would like to **confess** in church, but there is no opportunity because it is Christmas Day.

B Dickens makes Mrs Joe an even **less sympathetic** character. She is **mean and hypocritical**, treating guests differently from Pip and Joe.

C There is no mention of a Christmas present for Pip. He is barely allowed to be a **child** in Mrs Joe's house.

KEY FORM: FIRST-PERSON NARRATIVE (A02)

Great Expectations is written in the first person which conveys a strong understanding of the way that Pip reacts to the events around him. Pip's misery as he is picked on throughout the Christmas meal is both physical and emotional: he is squeezed in at the table 'with the Pumblechookian elbow in my eye' and 'they wouldn't leave me alone' (p. 23). In this section Dickens also helps us understand the terror that Pip feels at his involvement with the convict and the consequences of stealing the food from the house. However, Dickens adds humour to these scenes, for example the absurd way Pip jumps at every sound: 'I thought I heard the file still going; but it was only a sheep bell' (p. 32). The contrast between the file and the sheep creates the humour.

CHECKPOINT 4 (A02)

How does Dickens make it seem that Pip's secret will be discovered?

CHECKPOINT 5 (A02)

Find an example of the way that Mrs Joe behaves differently in front of the guests.

CHECKPOINT 6 (A01)

How does Pip feel about stealing the food and drink?

CHAPTERS 7–8: PIP'S FIRST VISIT TO MISS HAVISHAM

SUMMARY

- A year passes; Pip is to be apprenticed to Joe when he is old enough.

- He attends an evening school in the village, run by Mr Wopsle's great-aunt. She sleeps through the lessons and Pip has largely to teach himself to read, write and do simple sums.

- Pip writes a letter, in very basic English, to Joe. This leads to Joe telling Pip about his own difficult childhood with a drunken father who beat Joe and his mother.

- Mrs Joe announces that the rich but mysterious Miss Havisham has asked Pip to play at her house.

- Pip is quite literally (and violently) scrubbed down and sent off with Pumblechook to Miss Havisham the following morning where he meets Estella for the first time.

- Estella leads him by candlelight to the room in which Miss Havisham sits. Miss Havisham is dressed as a bride but everything in the room has aged and faded, including her.

- All the watches and clocks in the room have stopped at twenty minutes to nine.

CHECKPOINT 7   **A02**

How does Dickens introduce mystery around Miss Havisham?

WHY ARE THESE CHAPTERS IMPORTANT?

A   Learning to read and **education** in general is a **theme** throughout the **novel**.

B   The **first meeting with Miss Havisham** is a memorable and significant moment for Pip because it will change the course of his life.

C   Despite her **cruelty**, Pip falls in love with the young Estella.

CHECKPOINT 8   **A01**

Estella is cruel, but she is also lonely herself. Who might have affected her character?

EXAM FOCUS: EVALUATING CHARACTER (A02)

You may be asked to write about a particular character in depth and higher level answers demonstrate an ability to write about the less obvious details. The following is a response to a question about Pip's relationship with Joe, using evidence from this chapter to demonstrate a deeper understanding of Joe's character:

> When Pip begins to learn to read it reminds Joe of his own troubled childhood. It is because of this experience that Joe is so tolerant of his wife, of whom he says 'your sister is a fine figure of a woman' (p. 45). He does not want to find himself behaving like his own father has done. Joe does not condemn his father for the years of brutality, but insists that the man had a good 'hart' (p. 44). This is Dickens's way of presenting Joe as a very tolerant and forgiving man. Pip admires Joe for this and it could be argued that this experience plays a part in Pip's later forgiveness for his mistreatment by Miss Havisham and Mrs Joe.

Selects excellent quote for analysis of Joe

*Insightful comment showing awareness of links between Joe, Magwitch, Pip and Estella as **characters** that have had traumatic childhoods*

*Uses modal **verb** 'could be' to suggest a possible inference*

Now you try it:

Find an example of the way that Joe defends Pip against Mrs Joe. Start: *Joe often has to intervene or warn Pip when Mrs Joe loses her temper...*

KEY CONTEXT (A03)

Dickens is deliberately vague about Miss Havisham's past but this is typical of his writing style. His **novels** are full of secrets and mysteries.

KEY QUOTATION: PIP AND MISS HAVISHAM (A02)

The relationship between Pip and Miss Havisham is complex and ambiguous. Miss Havisham is motivated by her misery and humiliation at being jilted at the altar to take revenge on all men. This leads her to adopt Estella to be her instrument of revenge. Miss Havisham tells Pip: 'I have a sick fancy that I want to see some play' (p. 56). Estella plays cards with Pip and humiliates him repeatedly. Estella is happy that she is able to make him cry and Pip feels ignorant and resents his simple upbringing. Pip is captivated by Estella's beauty but does not know how to handle the cruelty she shows him. Although Miss Havisham is in some ways very open about her 'sick' nature, she also cruelly allows Pip to believe that she wants Pip to marry Estella, which had never actually been Miss Havisham's intention.

CHAPTERS 9–10: AN UNLIKELY TALE AND A MYSTERIOUS STRANGER

SUMMARY

- Pip is concerned that if he says what Miss Havisham and Satis House are really like, people will form the wrong impression. He is bullied by Mrs Joe and Pumblechook and so decides to invent an elaborate story about his visit.

- His description of the visit is ridiculous but he later tells the truth to Joe.

- In the Three Jolly Bargemen pub Pip encounters a mysterious stranger who appears to be stirring his drink with the file that Magwitch used to cut off his leg irons.

- The stranger both terrifies and bewilders Pip and leaves him with two pound notes, a large amount of money.

WHY ARE THESE CHAPTERS IMPORTANT?

A We see the young Pip's **sensitivity and kindness** towards Miss Havisham through the way that he lies about her to Pumblechook and Mrs Joe. He does not want them to know about the sad and upsetting details of the life she leads.

B The mysterious stranger (who we find out much later is an **acquaintance of Magwitch**) is Dickens's way of **developing** the different **plots** that take the reader through the novel.

C The money that the stranger leaves behind disturbs Pip – the **power of money** to change Pip's behaviour is a common theme in *Great Expectations*.

KEY SETTING: SATIS HOUSE (A03)

Satis House is one of the most memorable and famous fictional settings in all of Dickens's novels. Its decaying furniture, mouldering wedding cake, overgrown garden, flickering candles and scuttling rats and insects are Gothic in style. It can be seen as a physical representation of Miss Havisham's devastated mind as well as a reminder of one of the central themes of the novel – how greed and selfishness can ruin lives.

CHECKPOINT 9 (A01)

How has Pip been affected by Estella?

TOP TIP (A02)

Remember that instead of rejecting the strangers at Satis House, Pip shows an affinity for them and is happy to distance himself from those who have bullied him for most of his life.

CHAPTER 11: A SECOND VISIT TO SATIS HOUSE

SUMMARY

- On his second visit to Satis House, Estella taunts Pip as she leads him to Miss Havisham's room. She makes Pip say that she is pretty and then insults him.
- Pip passes Jaggers on the stairs but does not know who he is.
- The Pockets are also visiting, and they attempt to outdo one another in their efforts to impress Miss Havisham on her birthday, though she refuses to celebrate it.
- Pip explores the run-down grounds of the house and meets a boy of his own age, who insists that they should fight. We learn later that this is Herbert Pocket.
- A boxing match takes place and Pip easily beats the other boy, who keeps on fighting until he has almost been knocked out.
- Estella seems to have been watching and she appears to be pleased with Pip. She lets Pip kiss her on the cheek as he leaves.

CHECKPOINT 10 (A01)

Why does the first appearance of Jaggers need to be memorable?

WHY IS THIS CHAPTER IMPORTANT?

A This chapter gives us more examples of the way that **wealth** leads people such as Miss Havisham and the Pockets to behave in greedy and unpleasant ways.

B We learn more details about the **trauma and unhappiness** that Miss Havisham lives with, which also has a terrible **impact** on Estella. We also see Miss Havisham's deepening affection for Pip.

C The **friendship** between Pip and Herbert begins ironically with a fight, but Herbert becomes as important to Pip as Joe and Wemmick by the end of the novel.

KEY QUOTATION: PIP AND HERBERT POCKET (A02)

CHECKPOINT 11 (A01)

Why do Miss Havisham's visitors not dare to contradict their host, even when this makes them look foolish?

Herbert Pocket is a helpful character when you are writing about Pip because he provides some interesting contrasts. At this point in the novel both Herbert and Pip have been drawn into the unhappy world of Miss Havisham and Estella. The fight is Herbert's way of attempting to impress Estella. When Herbert challenges Pip, the adult narrator Pip asks: 'What could I do but follow him? I have often asked myself the same question since: but, what else could I do?' (p. 87). This shows Pip's lack of control over his experiences at Satis House. Herbert later talks about Estella and Miss Havisham with a mixture of horror and humour. Pip, in contrast, is drawn ever deeper into their world, partly due to his sensitivity to and compassion for their pain.

EXAM FOCUS: WRITING ABOUT MISS HAVISHAM

You may be asked to write about the ways that characters are presented in the novel. Read this example by one student examining the characterisation of Miss Havisham:

> *Focuses on Dickens's words and techniques*

Miss Havisham says that the Pockets will one day 'feast upon her' (p. 85). Dickens uses the gruesome cannibalism image as a metaphor for the money they hope to inherit from her. The visitors have come to see Miss Havisham because it is her birthday but instead Miss Havisham talks about her death and says that when she is laid out 'in my bride's dress' (p. 86) for her funeral, it will be the finished curse upon him' (p. 86) though she does not explain who this 'he' actually is. In fact, Miss Havisham was to have been married on her birthday. The coincidence of these two supposedly happy days creates more pathos when we see what she has become.

> *Helpful use of short, embedded quotation*

> *A specific literary term that means 'creating sympathy', correctly used*

Now you try it:

Find one more quotation that describes Miss Havisham and write a sentence explaining what language feature Dickens has used in the quotation, for example a metaphor. Start: *Dickens describes Miss Havisham as 'looking like the Witch of the place'. The word 'witch' could symbolise many aspects of Miss Havisham...*

TOP TIP A01

Show understanding of language by commenting on the ironic nature of the name 'Satis House'. There is no satisfaction there for anyone.

CHAPTERS 12–14: PIP BECOMES JOE'S APPRENTICE

SUMMARY

- Pip fears that he will be punished for hurting the boy with whom he fought at Satis House. He returns nervously to the house and pushes Miss Havisham around in her chair.
- He continues to call every other day at noon for eight to ten months. Pip tells Miss Havisham about the plans for him to be apprenticed to Joe as a blacksmith.
- Estella continues to treat Pip with disdain, though sometimes she is quite friendly towards him which confuses him.
- Miss Havisham asks Pip to bring Joe to see her so that the matter of Pip's apprenticeship can be settled. Pip grows increasingly irritated by Pumblechook's interference.
- Joe and Pip visit Satis House and are shown in by Estella, who takes no notice of either of them. Throughout the conversation with Miss Havisham, Joe addresses Pip instead of her.
- Miss Havisham gives Joe twenty-five guineas to pay for Pip to be apprenticed to him and she makes Joe agree that he will not look for any more money from her. Pip is told that he is not to visit again.

CHECKPOINT 12 (A02)

Even though Miss Havisham helps Pip, she allows Estella to behave badly. Why is this?

KEY CONTEXT (A03)

Miss Havisham pays Joe in guineas, which went out of circulation in 1817. They were still legal tender but show Miss Havisham's old-fashioned ways.

WHY ARE THESE CHAPTERS IMPORTANT?

A We learn that Pip's **future** does not appear to lie with Miss Havisham and Estella because he will be an apprentice blacksmith. Pip is not satisfied with this trade but has no choice.

B The interactions between Miss Havisham and Joe are typical of Dickens's **humour** and tendency to include **eccentric characters** in his work.

C We continue to see Pip's deepening affection for Estella despite her **cold and distant manner**.

KEY LANGUAGE: CRUELTY AND UNKINDNESS (A02)

There are many occasions in the **novel** when Dickens makes characters speak in cruel and thoughtless ways and these chapters have several examples. Miss Havisham seems to take great delight in Estella's ability to captivate Pip, using **hyperbolic** language to urge Estella to 'break their hearts and give no mercy!' (p. 92). Miss Havisham cruelly dismisses Pip with the blunt, direct statement 'Gargery is your master now' (p. 98). Pumblechook and Mrs Joe treat Pip cruelly and Pip says his sister would speak to him 'as if she was morally wrenching one of my teeth out at every reference' (p. 93), a disturbingly violent **metaphorical image** to describe her behaviour towards Pip.

TOP TIP: WRITING ABOUT MARRIAGE IN *GREAT EXPECTATIONS* (A02)

Unhappy marriages are common in *Great Expectations*. Miss Havisham was badly treated regarding marriage; being abandoned on the day of her wedding has caused huge emotional damage, much of which is then passed onto Estella. Estella's short marriage to Bentley Drummle is full of violence and fear, as is the marriage between Mrs Joe and Joe. Wemmick and Herbert both have happy marriages, but these have less significance in the novel. It is worth remembering that Dickens explored his feelings about marriage in many of his novels, sometimes presenting marriage as a wonderful state, sometimes as a disaster, which reflected his own mixed experiences.

REVISION FOCUS: SATIS HOUSE

- Make a list of the **Gothic** features of Satis House in this chapter, such as the stopped clocks and the snow, all of which Dickens uses to create a dark and mysterious atmosphere.

- You could draw a plan or map of the house and label it with these features to help you remember as many details as possible in the exam.

CHECKPOINT 13 (A02)

How are Pip's feelings towards Joe changing?

CHAPTER 15: ORLICK CAUSES TROUBLE AND MRS JOE IS ATTACKED

SUMMARY

- Pip continues his limited education under Biddy and Wopsle.
- We are introduced to Orlick, Joe's awkward and aggressive assistant worker at the forge.
- When Pip asks for a half-holiday, Orlick insists that he should have one too. Joe agrees, but his wife scolds him for being weak, leading to an argument between Orlick and Mrs Joe. Joe and Orlick fight but Joe wins easily.
- Pip visits Satis House where Sarah Pocket admits him reluctantly. Miss Havisham tells Pip that Estella is abroad, being educated. Miss Havisham continues to be cruel to Pip, despite his friendly intentions.
- On the way home, Pip meets Wopsle and is persuaded to join him and Pumblechook for the evening.
- When they head for home they come across Orlick who is waiting beside the road and says he has been to London. He points out that the guns at the hulks are firing, showing that a prisoner has escaped.
- On returning to the forge, Pip finds his sister unconscious. The argument and the fight put Orlick under suspicion.

WHY IS THIS CHAPTER IMPORTANT?

A   This chapter introduces an **important minor character**, Orlick.

B   Pip's ongoing **connection** to Miss Havisham often brings him disappointment and sadness.

C   The **attack** on Mrs Joe is mysterious and unexpected. Orlick avoids capture and punishment for this vicious act, and does not admit that he carried it out until close to the end of the **novel** in Chapter 53.

CHECKPOINT 14 **A02**

Orlick is described in an unsympathetic way. For example, he is constantly referred to as 'slouching' (p. 114). Why is this?

TOP TIP **A02**

Make sure you can write about how the attack on Mrs Joe marks a definite stage in Pip's life. From this point onward there is no one to hold Pip back from leaving the forge.

EXAM FOCUS: WRITING ABOUT ORLICK

A02

You may have a question that asks you to write about one of the more minor characters in *Great Expectations*, such as Orlick. Read this student's response to a question about Orlick's role:

> Orlick is a bad-tempered young man who resents Pip's appearance in the forge. Dickens often uses verbs such as 'growled' (p. 110) to show how Orlick speaks. Orlick threatens to 'choke' Mrs Joe (p. 111). He is untrustworthy and says that his first name is 'Dolge', but Pip thinks this unlikely (p. 108). It is sometimes suggested that Orlick is like Pip's 'evil twin'. Orlick always wants to have whatever Pip has, for example, when Pip asks for a half-holiday, Orlick insists that he should have one too. It could also be argued that when Orlick fatally attacks Mrs Joe, he is actually just doing something that Pip himself might have liked to do. However, Pip and Orlick are very different in many ways.

Use of an appropriate language term

Shows awareness of different interpretations of a character

Connective at start of sentence helps to signal change in the argument

Now you try it:

Add a sentence or two explaining the ways that Orlick and Pip are different, using one or two quotations from the novel to back up your points. Start: *Although Pip and Orlick come from the same geographical background, their personalities and attitudes are vastly different...*

KEY QUOTATION: JOE'S DEFENCE OF MRS JOE **A02**

Orlick rudely criticises Mrs Joe's bad temper, saying: 'if you was my wife[,] I'd hold you under the pump, and choke it out of you' (p. 111). Mrs Joe goes into a frenzy of anger. Joe is faced with no choice but to confront Orlick. This leads to a surprising scene about which Pip comments: 'if any man in that neighbourhood could stand up long against Joe, I never saw the man' (p. 111). This reminds us of Joe's great strength; he wins the fight with Orlick easily. Joe is described as physically carrying Mrs Joe into the house, which descends into a 'singular calm and silence' (p. 112) as a result of Joe's powerful presence. A successful exam response about Joe Gargery could refer to this less obvious side of his personality.

TOP TIP **A02**

Dickens has set up the final part of the novel here as the reader knows that Orlick bears a grudge against Pip and that he can be violent. Make sure you understand how the relationship between Pip and Orlick is an important part of the structure of the novel.

CHAPTERS 16–17: MRS JOE FAILS TO RECOVER AND PIP CONFIDES IN BIDDY

SUMMARY

- Pip gets a clearer picture of Mrs Joe's attack. Before nine o'clock, a farm labourer had seen her in the doorway of the kitchen. Joe was in the Three Jolly Bargemen. When Joe returned home at five to ten Mrs Joe was on the floor.
- Mrs Joe had been struck with something heavy. There was a convict's leg-iron on the floor next to her. Pip is sure that it is his convict's iron, and is frightened.
- Pip suspects Orlick but neither Pip nor the constables find any evidence for this and no one is arrested.
- Mrs Joe does not recover from her injuries. She is left unable to speak and seems to understand little of what is said to her. Biddy joins the household to help out.
- Mrs Joe traces out what appears to be a capital letter T, which puzzles everyone. Eventually Biddy realises that it is a hammer and is meant to represent Orlick but there is nothing anyone can do.
- Orlick remains working at the forge and, strangely, appears to be favoured by Mrs Joe.
- Pip carries on his apprenticeship at the forge but visits Miss Havisham on his birthday. He later confides in Biddy that 'I want to be a gentleman' (p. 124) and wishes to lead a very different life.
- He also suggests that he wishes he could fall in love with Biddy, but is too preoccupied with Estella, however cruel she may be.

CHECKPOINT 15 A01

Why is it important that suspicion should fall on Orlick?

CHECKPOINT 16 A01

Who could have placed the convict's leg-iron in the farmhouse?

WHY ARE THESE CHAPTERS IMPORTANT?

A Mrs Joe's terrible injuries mean she is no longer a barrier to Pip's **ambitions**.

B The conversation between Pip and Biddy is the first time Pip openly expresses his desire to be a **gentleman**.

C We can see Pip's **confusion**, or 'perplexities' (p. 129), over his ambitions to leave the forge weighed against his **loyalty and gratitude** to Joe.

KEY LANGUAGE: HOW DICKENS CONVEYS FEELINGS

Dickens often draws our attention to small details to bring to life the way a **character** is thinking or feeling. During his conversation with Biddy about his ambition, Pip experiences a range of conflicting emotions, some of which are subtly characterised by the way he plays with the blades of grass on the river bank. When he is anxious, Pip is shown 'plucking' at the grass as if he 'pulled [his] feelings out of [his] hair' (p. 124). Later, calling himself a 'lunatic' because of his feelings for Estella, Pip throws the grass into the river 'as if [he] had some thoughts of following it' (p.125): Dickens makes Pip's actions mirror his desperate feelings.

> ### KEY CONTEXT   A03
>
> Note that despite her obvious intelligence, there would have been little possibility of Biddy leaving the forge for a better life. Women had fewer rights and opportunities at that time, being unable to vote or attend university, for example.

AIMING HIGH: COMMENTING ON TONE

Tone is a helpful word to describe the atmosphere or feeling created at any point in a story. Throughout *Great Expectations*, there are frequent changes in tone from horror to the surreal, the everyday, the mysterious and so on. This can happen within the same chapter, from paragraph to paragraph, and being aware of this variety of tone is essential to showing that you understand Dickens at the highest level. For example, in Chapter 17 the tone of the scene between Pip and Biddy is thoughtful and moving. This then gives way to the dark humour of the meeting with Orlick: Pip reflects on one of Orlick's more ludicrous coinages, 'jiggered', claiming that Orlick makes up such words to 'affront mankind' (p.128). Dickens is using **hyperbole** and humour here to convey the tone of grim acceptance that Pip is forced into and so creates a different tone from the preceding paragraphs.

CHAPTERS 18–19: PIP IS TO BECOME A GENTLEMAN

SUMMARY

- Pip, in the fourth year of his apprenticeship, meets a mysterious stranger at the Three Jolly Bargemen pub, whom he recognises as the man who passed him on the stairs of Satis House (in Chapter 11).
- The man asks to speak privately to Joe and Pip, and introduces himself as Mr Jaggers, a lawyer from London.
- Mr Jaggers tells Pip that he has great expectations and must begin his education as a gentleman at once. Joe agrees to release the boy from his indentures. Jaggers says Pip may not know the name of his benefactor, although Pip is sure it is Miss Havisham.
- Pip is impatient to leave for London to begin his new life. He tells Biddy he would like Joe to visit him in London, but that he is worried Joe might seem out of place.
- Pip has a new suit made at Trabb's and visits Miss Havisham. He interprets everything that Miss Havisham says to mean that she has given him the money and opportunity to be a gentleman, even though her cruelty towards him makes this unlikely.
- Pip finally leaves for London.

WHY ARE THESE CHAPTERS IMPORTANT?

A   This is the first time we learn about Pip's **benefactor**.

B   Pip continues to **distance himself** from the people around him in Kent, with his newly acquired wealth giving him more reason to see himself as superior.

C   Pip's **incorrect belief** that Miss Havisham is paying for him to go to London begins in these chapters.

KEY QUOTATION: MORAL JUDGEMENTS (A03)

Biddy continues to be a moral compass in Pip's life: she always knows right from wrong, even if Pip chooses to ignore her. Pip accuses her of being jealous of his new wealth, but Biddy refuses to defend herself against such a ludicrous suggestion. Instead she says: 'a gentleman should not be unjust' (p. 146). Throughout the rest of the novel Pip's treatment of Biddy and Joe is a measure of how he sees himself as a 'gentleman' and whether he behaves in a 'just' or 'fair' way to people around him.

CHECKPOINT 17 (A01)

What conclusion does Pip jump to regarding Miss Havisham?

REVISION FOCUS: CLOTHING AND CHARACTER

Pip's visit to Trabb's the tailors is a **symbolic** moment in his journey towards being a gentleman, as he is aware of the importance of wearing the clothes that show his new status and wealth. Clothes are significant throughout the novel. For each main **character**, look for something notable about their clothing – Mrs Joe's apron, Miss Havisham's single shoe, Herbert's bow tie, for example – and list two things that it tells us about that character.

TOP TIP (A02)

Look at Trabb, Trabb's boy and Pumblechook. Their behaviour typifies some of the different ways that people respond to Pip's wealth.

CHECKPOINT 18 (A02)

How is Pip's immaturity revealed in the conversation with Miss Havisham?

EXAM FOCUS: WRITING ABOUT THE NOVEL'S STRUCTURE (A02)

You may be asked to write about the way that Dickens has structured the novel because it is one of the key techniques that writers use. Read this successful response in which the student has explained some of the ways that Dickens uses structure for particular effects:

Shows understanding of the historical context with clear link to the novel

Because Dickens originally wrote 'Great Expectations' to sell one chapter at a time, it was important that each chapter left the reader wanting to read on. This means that the plot had to have lots of mysteries to be solved. Dickens deliberately withholds the identity of Pip's benefactor despite the fact that we know the adult Pip is the narrator of the story as he looks back on his life. At the end of Chapter 19, Pip comments 'the mists had all solemnly risen now, and the world lay spread before me' (p. 157) which contains a metaphor for Pip's journey into adult life (the 'rising' mist) but also has a tone of excitement and mystery which makes the reader want to continue to the next chapter.

Uses a range of vocabulary

Correct technical term

Now you try it:

Take another chapter in the novel and note down what happens at the beginning, middle and end. Look for the details that make the reader ask what might happen next. Start: *Chapter 15 begins with Pip discussing Miss Havisham with Joe...*

CHAPTERS 20–2: PIP LEAVES FOR LONDON

SUMMARY

- Pip arrives in London and visits Mr Jaggers's office and dismal surrounding area.
- Back at Jaggers's he sees how the lawyer deals with his clients in a firm and sometimes brutal manner. Jaggers explains Pip's allowance and says he will try to keep Pip out of debt.
- Wemmick takes Pip to Barnard's Inn which is a shabby collection of rooms and apartments. After showing Pip round and trying to make him feel at home, the young man, Herbert, recognises Pip.
- Herbert tells Pip that Estella was adopted by Miss Havisham and has been brought up to exact revenge on the male sex. He also tells him that Mr Jaggers is Miss Havisham's lawyer.
- Pip asks Herbert to put him straight about London manners. Herbert gives Pip the name Handel, after the composer who wrote 'The Harmonious Blacksmith'.
- Herbert tells Pip that many years before, Miss Havisham had been jilted on her wedding day: 'At that hour and minute ... she afterwards stopped all the clocks' (p. 176). She had let the house go to ruin and had not seen daylight since.
- Herbert shows Pip around London and on the Monday he takes him to his parents' chaotic house at Hammersmith.

KEY CONTEXT

Dickens's *Bleak House* (1853) has a long-running court case at its centre. Just as in *Great Expectations*, Dickens shows the legal system ruining many people's lives.

CHECKPOINT 19 (A03)

What does Jaggers's behaviour tell you about the law?

WHY ARE THESE CHAPTERS IMPORTANT?

A They introduce a **new setting**, busy central London, which contrasts greatly with the quiet and desolate Kent marshes.

B We see the reality of the **law courts** and Jaggers's life as a **criminal lawyer**.

C Pip's important **friendship** with Herbert Pocket begins and Herbert tells Pip some of the details of **Miss Havisham's past**.

TOP TIP: WRITING ABOUT THE LEGAL SYSTEM

Pip's first impressions of London are coloured by the gallows and the criminal law business. Dickens includes his own negative views on British law here. He often wrote about the expensive and ruinous procedures of the English legal proceedings, and he was involved with legal proceedings throughout his life, helping his father with his legal troubles and fighting cases about the copyright of his works. You should remember that Dickens disliked lawyers and courts and was highly suspicious of them.

KEY SETTING: LONDON (A02)

Pip has long dreamed of leaving the forge and making his way in the city. However, Dickens makes it clear that Pip's dreams are impossibly romantic and the reality of London is often horrific. Dickens uses a multi-sensory approach to bring London to life for the reader. He describes the 'hot, exhausted air' (p. 159), the 'filth and fat and blood' of the Smithfield meat market, the 'noise of passing vehicles' and the people Pip encounters at Newgate Prison as 'smelling strongly of spirits and beer' (p. 160). Pip uses a range of adjectives to describe his response to the city, such as 'dreadful' and 'sickening' (p. 160). It is worth remembering that Pip does grow used to the city and so these first impressions possibly also serve to reflect his bewilderment at what is a strange new place for him.

KEY QUOTATION: WHAT IS A GENTLEMAN? (A01)

Dickens uses the **character** of Herbert Pocket to explore 'What is a gentleman?' Herbert says to Pip: 'no man who was not a true gentleman at heart, ever was, since the world began, a true gentleman in manner' (p.175). This draws an important distinction that is explored in the **novel**: being a 'gentleman' does not just mean wearing fine clothes and being rich – it is a way of behaving. Ultimately, Pip learns that good people such as Wemmick, Herbert and Joe are true 'gentlemen' despite their relative lack of money. They contrast greatly with Compeyson and Drummle, who are wealthy but cruel and violent.

AIMING HIGH: RECOGNISING AND COMMENTING ON HUMOUR ⭐

It can be difficult to see the humour and jokes in texts such as *Great Expectations* because they may depend on understanding specific social history. However, a successful candidate should be able to see the humour in *Great Expectations*, because this is an important aspect of Dickens's writing and shows close understanding. Even in the darkest moments, Dickens can make us smile. His description of Pip's first visit to a city office (which should be a momentous experience for him) is full of absurd and funny details, such as the 'young Insurers'

who appear to have been incubated in 'the eggs of ostriches' and the gravy on the tables at the 'celebrated house' (p. 180) about which Pip had previously had such grand ideas. Humour is also to be found in the descriptions of Wemmick's home at Walworth and, more darkly, in the exchanges between Miss Havisham and the Pockets.

TOP TIP (A02)

Notice how Dickens uses Herbert as a **narrator** to fill in the gaps in our knowledge about Miss Havisham.

TOP TIP (A02)

Beware red herrings! The belief that Miss Havisham is Pip's benefactor seems to be confirmed by the connection between her and Jaggers. Herbert seems to be of the same opinion.

CHAPTERS 23–5: PIP MEETS NEW PEOPLE

SUMMARY

- The Pocket household with its seven children is chaotic, appearing to be run by and for the servants. Mrs Pocket takes little notice of what goes on around her. Mr Pocket welcomes Pip. He has two other boarding pupils, Startop and Bentley Drummle.

- Pip settles in at the Pocket house but keeps his room at Barnard's. He goes to see Mr Jaggers who provides him with money to buy furniture although Pip finds dealing with Jaggers uncomfortable. Pip begins to fall into debt.

- At Wemmick's suggestion they go to a police court to watch Mr Jaggers at work. Pip gets the impression that everyone there is terrified of Jaggers, even the magistrates.

- At Hammersmith, Pip enjoys rowing on the river with Herbert and the other two pupils. He finds Drummle surly and proud and prefers the company of the gentler Startop.

- Pip goes to Wemmick's home in Walworth one evening. He is surprised to find that the house is a little wooden building like a toy castle, complete with drawbridge, flagpole and a small cannon. Wemmick asks Pip not to mention his home life to Jaggers as he likes to keep the office and the Castle separate.

WHY ARE THESE CHAPTERS IMPORTANT?

A Bentley Drummle plays a **major role** in Pip's life as he later marries and violently abuses Estella.

B Pip is settling in well but **spending too much money**.

C Wemmick is a **gentle and friendly influence** in Pip's life.

CHECKPOINT 20 A01

What purpose does the visit to Wemmick's house serve?

CHECKPOINT 21 A02

How does Wemmick change when he is at home?

KEY CONTEXT A03

Wemmick's make-believe world is in stark contrast to the harsh reality of life in London and he becomes a completely different **character** when he is away from the oppressive atmosphere of Mr Jaggers's office.

EXAM FOCUS: WRITING ABOUT PIP AS NARRATOR (A02)

Great Expectations is a first-person **novel** with Pip as the **narrator**. This successful student response contains comments about the kind of language Pip uses:

> **Appropriate technical term**

Pip is a biased narrator who tells the story very much from his point of view. For example, his descriptions of Bentley Drummle concentrate very much on Drummle's negative points even before Drummle has met and married Estella. Pip uses a humorous image, saying Drummle 'was so sulky a fellow that he even took up a book as if its writer had done him an injury (p. 197). Pip describes Drummle as 'sluggish' and 'proud' and says that he creeps around 'like some uncomfortable amphibious creature' (p. 198), suggesting that Drummle is ugly, slow and toad-like, for example. Dickens does not show Pip trying to find something positive about Drummle in any way.

> **Recognises subtle tone created as part of Pip's narratorial voice**

> **Explores connotations of imagery fully**

Now you try it:

Find a sentence in the novel where Pip describes a character he likes – Herbert, for example – and note down how Pip's choice of language and use of **imagery** change to express his different feelings about that person. Start: *In contrast, Pip feels warmth and affection for Herbert...*

TOP TIP (A03)

Watch David Lean's film of another novel by Dickens, *Oliver Twist* (1948), for an insight into the life of the criminal world in London.

CHAPTERS 26–8: DINNER WITH JAGGERS

SUMMARY

- Jaggers invites Pip to dine with him the following evening and tells him to bring Herbert, Drummle and Startop. They all meet at the lawyer's office and Jaggers conducts them to his house in Soho.
- After Drummle has been boasting about his strength Jaggers makes his housekeeper, Molly, show her wrists, much against her will. He tells them he has never known a stronger grip in man or woman.
- Drummle becomes increasingly rude and unpleasant. Jaggers later tells Pip that he likes 'the Spider' but that Pip should stay clear of him.
- About a month later, Drummle finishes his tuition at Mr Pocket's and goes home.
- Pip receives a letter from Biddy to say that Joe is coming to London with Mr Wopsle and would like to visit him. Joe's visit is embarrassing and awkward as the blacksmith feels completely out of place. Joe delivers a message from Miss Havisham that Estella has come home and would like to see Pip.
- The next day Pip sets out for home. At first he intends to stay with Joe and Biddy but decides instead to stay at the Blue Boar.
- Two convicts are on the coach going to the prison ships. Pip is horrified when he recognises one of them as the man who gave him two pound notes in the Three Jolly Bargemen one Saturday night.
- Pip overhears him explaining how another convict had asked him to give the two pounds to a boy who had fed him and kept his secret when he escaped once in Kent.
- Pip gets off the coach as soon as it reaches town and goes to the Blue Boar. The incident makes him realise how easily he could be exposed as somebody who helped a convict to escape capture.

CHECKPOINT 22 (A02)

Why might Jaggers seem fascinated by the surly Drummle and call him 'the Spider'?

WHY ARE THESE CHAPTERS IMPORTANT?

A We are introduced to **Molly** (Estella's birth mother).

B We see Pip's increasing **snobbery**.

C Dickens reminds us of the convict from Pip's childhood: the **plot revelation** involving the full **identities** of Molly, Estella and Magwitch is gradually being developed.

KEY CHARACTER: JAGGERS (A02)

As happens throughout the **novel**, Pip is able to see the different sides of his friends and acquaintances and how they behave both professionally and in private. Here we get a glimpse of Jaggers at home. Pip is puzzled by Jaggers's interest in Drummle whom he names 'the Spider' (p. 206). Pip feels that Jaggers has a talent for discovering the worst sides of people's characters. He observes Jaggers's housekeeper whom Wemmick describes as 'a wild beast tamed' (p. 202).

> **KEY CONTEXT** (A03)
>
> Victorian prisons were overcrowded and ships were regularly used to house prisoners. Dickens took part in a campaign against such inhumane punishments.

> **TOP TIP** (A01)
>
> Always show you are aware of Dickens developing the plot: Pip's unpleasant reminder of the convict on the marshes prepares the reader for the appearance of Magwitch.

TOP TIP: WRITING ABOUT DICKENS'S LANGUAGE (A01)

Joe's visit to London enables Dickens to write a scene that is both funny, as in the extended **imagery** of how Joe handles his hat like a 'bird's-nest' (p. 214), but also sad, because it shows the gap between Pip and Joe. For Joe's way of speaking, Dickens uses **dialect** words, e.g. 'ever right' for 'always right' (p. 214), and non-standard spelling, e.g. 'werry' for 'very' and 'calc'lated' for 'calculated' (p. 215) to show Joe's rural accent. Although Pip grew up in the same place as Joe, he learns not to use this local dialect. You could make a link between this scene and Chapter 8 in which Pip is laughed at by Estella for the different language that he uses, e.g. 'Jacks' for 'knaves' in a pack of cards, which Estella thinks is 'coarse' (p. 58).

REVISION FOCUS: PIP AND JOE

In Chapter 27, Joe is clumsy and confused and he upsets Pip by calling him 'Sir' (p. 215). Pip has become a snob and has begun to deceive himself. Joe refuses Pip's invitation to dinner and suggests that Pip would see him in a better light if he visited him at the forge.

Make a timeline of the relationship between Pip and Joe, and note at each point the attitude Pip displays towards Joe, such as admiration, friendship, gratitude, shame, embarrassment and so on. Who changes, Pip or Joe?

CHAPTERS 29–31: PIP AND ESTELLA MEET AGAIN

SUMMARY

- In the morning, Pip goes to Satis House and is unpleasantly surprised to find that Orlick is employed there as gatekeeper. Sarah Pocket is also at the house.
- When Pip goes into Miss Havisham's room he does not immediately recognise the elegant lady who is sitting next to her: it is Estella, more beautiful than ever.
- Miss Havisham encourages them to walk in the garden together and they talk of old times. Pip is puzzled by something, but cannot work out what it is. Estella warns Pip that she has no heart. Pip is still convinced that Miss Havisham intends that they should be married.
- Mr Jaggers arrives, to Pip's surprise. At dinner Jaggers is very quiet and avoids looking at Estella. It is arranged that Pip will meet Estella at the coach when she travels to London.
- Pip does not visit Joe, as he imagines Estella would not approve of him keeping up such lowly connections.
- On the next day, Pip tells Jaggers of his misgivings about Orlick, and Jaggers says he will sack him. Pip is mocked by Trabb's boy.
- They attend Wopsle's performance of *Hamlet* which is incompetent and ridiculous. The actors are frequently interrupted and insulted by members of the audience.

WHY ARE THESE CHAPTERS IMPORTANT?

A We see Pip's feelings for Estella develop into a more **adult, romantic attraction**.

B Pip is still **deceived** about the connections between Miss Havisham, Estella and Jaggers.

C Dickens includes some humour with another **deluded** character, Mr Wopsle.

KEY STRUCTURE: MISS HAVISHAM'S DECEPTION

As Pip walks around the garden at Satis House with Estella, he comments: 'I felt that our patroness had chosen us for one another. Wretched boy!' (p. 233). The reader knows it is the grown-up Pip looking back on his life writing this, showing how much pain the misunderstanding has caused him. This also makes the final scenes between Pip and the dying Miss Havisham in Chapter 49, in which he forgives her for this cruelty, so much more poignant and powerful.

KEY CONTEXT **A03**

Although the scenes involving Wopsle's play seem out of place, this is a typical piece of humorous writing by Dickens that would have been very popular with his audiences.

CHECKPOINT 23 **A02**

Why has Pip ignored all warnings about Estella?

AIMING HIGH: WRITING ABOUT SOCIAL POSITION ⭐

The highest scoring answers will show a strong understanding of some of the complex Victorian social structures that Dickens describes in the **novel**. Herbert may not be rich, but his family has good social connections and he is a typical gentleman whose advice is very important for Pip. You may have an opportunity to explore the difference in status between Pip and Herbert: when Herbert confides to Pip that he is secretly engaged to a young woman called Clara who lives with her invalid father, he fears that his mother would not approve of the girl's social position. The best answers will show that many of the characters do not have a clear or stable social position. Estella, for example, may have wealth, education and connections, but is the biological daughter of two criminals and so her social position is complicated.

KEY QUOTATION: TRABB'S BOY (A02)

Although these chapters develop the story about Pip and Estella, Dickens constantly reminds us that Pip's struggle to become a gentleman can lead him into some humorous and even bizarre scenes. Pip is chased along the road by Trabb the tailor's boy, whom Pip first encounters in Chapter 19. Trabb's boy shouts, 'Don't know yah, don't know yah, pon my soul don't know yah!'; he **parodies** Pip's manner of walking so that Pip is mortified but feels he cannot retaliate as it would be 'futile and degrading' (p. 240). This small scene is Dickens's timely reminder to the reader of Pip's increasing distance from his humble background: once, he was at the very same level as Trabb's boy. In many ways, it is hard to understand who Pip is.

CHECKPOINT 24 (A02)

What does the visit to the play bring to the novel?

TOP TIP (A02)

Notice how Dickens often contrasts characters. Pip's hopeless love for Estella contrasts with Herbert's much more realistic love for Clara.

CHAPTERS 32–5: ESTELLA VISITS PIP AND HIS SISTER DIES

SUMMARY

- Pip receives a message from Estella arranging to meet him in London the following day. Whilst in London, Wemmick shows Pip the shocking conditions of Newgate Prison.
- Pip takes Estella to Richmond. Her manner – a mixture of friendliness and distance – puzzles him, although he still believes they will marry one day.
- A letter informs Pip of Mrs Joe's death. Pip is angrily convinced that Orlick attacked her, but he has no proof. Pip travels to the forge for the funeral.
- Later Pip talks to Biddy and learns that she intends to be a teacher now that her work at the forge is ended. They talk about Pip's sister and about Orlick who, Biddy says, has been lurking around.

CHECKPOINT 25 **A02**

Pip senses a connection between Estella and Jaggers. What is this connection?

WHY ARE THESE CHAPTERS IMPORTANT?

A Pip's **feelings** about Estella continue to grow.

B The **death of Mrs Joe** is part of the plot that concerns Orlick's hatred for Pip.

C Pip is unaware of his **snobbish behaviour** around Joe and Biddy.

KEY FORM: DICKENS'S USE OF SATIRE (A02)

Dickens shows his exasperation with some of the more ridiculous Victorian customs and, in his description of Mrs Joe's funeral, he shows his skill in creating humour in tragic circumstances. The funeral is a grim **farce** organised by Trabb & Co. with professional mourners and lots of black crepe: Joe is 'entangled' (p. 273) in his overly complicated mourning outfit. One of the professional mourners is described as 'a carpenter who had once eaten two geese for a wager' (p. 273); such detail is typical of Dickens's use of **satire**, because it undercuts the serious nature of the mourner's role. Joe says he would have preferred a simpler and homely burial but puts his unthinking trust in the elaborate routines because he thinks that this shows more respect.

KEY CONTEXT (A03)

The Victorians were fascinated by death and organised elaborate funerals. Look at the ornate nature of Victorian graves in an old cemetery.

KEY QUOTATION: PIP, ESTELLA AND JAGGERS (A02)

In these chapters, Dickens continues to develop the story line that links Pip, Estella, Miss Havisham, Magwitch and Jaggers through many different ties. On the way to Richmond, Pip and Estella talk about Mr Jaggers and Pip experiences 'that inexplicable feeling I had had before' (p. 263). Pip's sensitivity to the impact that these people are having on his life is clear, even though he may not understand fully all the ways their lives are intertwined. As he thinks this, a gas light flashes brightly over Pip and Estella, perhaps **symbolising** the fact that one day everything will be fully revealed to Pip.

CHAPTERS 36–9: PIP'S BENEFACTOR IS REVEALED

SUMMARY

- Pip and Herbert continue to run up debts.
- Pip turns twenty-one. He asks Jaggers for information about his guardian but Jaggers only produces a five hundred pound note.
- Pip decides to help Herbert start in business. He has tea with Wemmick, his father and Wemmick's friend, Miss Skiffins. Wemmick agrees to help Pip set Herbert up in business, without Herbert's knowledge.
- Estella tells Pip that Miss Havisham wants to see him. At Satis House, Pip is disturbed by the way in which Miss Havisham is eager to know about the men who are fascinated by Estella. Pip witnesses a bitter quarrel between Miss Havisham and Estella.
- Back in London, Pip and Herbert go to a meeting of the dining club. Pip is angry at Drummle's proposal of a toast to Estella.
- Pip is twenty-three, and he and Herbert have moved to apartments in the Temple. One stormy night Pip hears footsteps on the stairs and a terrifying stranger emerges. Pip is shocked as the man discloses that he is his benefactor, and that Jaggers is his agent.
- After being transported to Australia, the convict whom Pip had helped on the marshes had made a great deal of money and had rewarded Pip by having him educated as a gentleman. Magwitch has returned to England to see his creation even though he may be hanged if he is caught in the country.
- Pip finds Magwitch repulsive but shelters him and gives him Herbert's bed. Pip realises that he had imagined Miss Havisham's plans for Estella and him and that he has abandoned Joe for the sake of a convict.

WHY ARE THESE CHAPTERS IMPORTANT?

- **A** Pip has a clearer understanding of **Estella's miserable life**.
- **B** Pip tries to help Herbert, showing his **kind side**.
- **C** The return of Magwitch turns Pip's **world upside down**.

KEY LANGUAGE: MAGWITCH RETURNS

Dickens uses many language features in order to create a suitable atmosphere and make the return of Magwitch memorable for the reader. He **personifies** the wind, saying it is so noisy it 'assailed and tore' at the sound of the church bells (p. 307). He **foregrounds** the appearance of Magwitch by comparing his footsteps to the 'the footstep of my dead sister' (p. 307) which is a typically **Gothic**, ghostly **image**. Magwitch's voice can be heard 'from the darkness beneath' (p. 308) which could be interpreted as a reference to hell (believed by some to be where terrible people go when they die). Magwitch addresses Pip as 'Mr Pip' and 'Master' (p. 308) to show his respect (although Pip finds this disturbing). Finally, Dickens uses non-standard spelling to represent Magwitch's rough speech, e.g. 'arterwards' for 'afterwards' (p. 309).

CHECKPOINT 26 (A01)

How does Pip show his generous nature at this point?

CHECKPOINT 27 (A01)

How does Miss Havisham seem at this point in the novel?

KEY CONTEXT (A03)

Transportation was a method of punishment that forced convicts to live the rest of their lives in another country, such as Australia or New Zealand.

AIMING HIGH: EXPLORING DIFFERENT INTERPRETATIONS OF MISS HAVISHAM

Miss Havisham is one of Dickens's most famous characters but the most successful answers to questions about her will show an ability to explore different interpretations, and provide evidence from the novel to back them up. Miss Havisham can be seen as a victim of cruelty but also as a perpetrator of terrible acts. When Estella asks 'Who taught me to be hard?' (p. 299), Dickens shows us that Estella's upbringing has caused her great emotional damage. However, Dickens hints that Miss Havisham is in turn disturbed by Estella's behaviour as Pip begins to see 'fear' (p. 301) in Miss Havisham's manner towards her.

REVISION FOCUS: KEY PLOT LINES

Notice how the various strands of the story are coming together. The reader is left wondering how the following points will be resolved.

- Estella's parentage
- Miss Havisham's future
- Pip and Estella
- The role of Magwitch in Pip's life
- Orlick's hatred of Pip

Draw a timeline of the main events in each character's life so that you have a clear understanding of their role in the novel.

CHECKPOINT 28 **A02**

How does Dickens use the weather to announce the arrival of Magwitch?

CHECKPOINT 29 **A01**

What does Pip now realise about his life so far?

TOP TIP: WRITING ABOUT THE AUTHOR **A02**

You will not get high marks simply by retelling the story: always add your own ideas about characters and themes as well as key quotations. Remember to refer to Dickens's style and techniques whenever you can. Answers that do not refer to Dickens as the writer will not show that you are 'analysing the effects used by the author', which is a key AO2 requirement. You should also refer to 'the reader' or to 'us'. Some useful sentence structures could be:

- In this chapter Dickens presents...
- Dickens shows the reader...
- By using this word [insert the quote you are writing about], Dickens helps us to understand...

CHAPTERS 40–2: MAGWITCH'S STORY

SUMMARY

- Pip tells everyone that the convict is his uncle. He is disturbed to find that someone may have followed the old man into the building.
- Pip calls on Jaggers, who confirms that Magwitch (who calls himself Provis) is indeed his benefactor.
- Herbert is surprised and shocked by Pip's guest and the news he has brought. Magwitch swears him to secrecy.
- Pip has arranged lodgings for Magwitch nearby and Herbert agrees that the most important thing is to get Magwitch out of the country.
- Pip feels that he cannot take any more of Magwitch's money and that his presence in England is a danger to them all. Pip and Herbert resolve to help him leave.
- Magwitch tell his story. He has been in and out of jails all his life and does not remember his parents. Twenty years ago he was the accomplice of a swindler and forger called Compeyson, who had been brought up as a gentleman but was now a criminal.
- Compeyson and Magwitch were arrested, but Compeyson betrayed Magwitch, who received a greater prison sentence. They both escaped on the marshes but Magwitch felt compelled to return Compeyson to captivity. Compeyson's punishment for escaping was light while Magwitch's was transportation for life.
- Herbert informs Pip that Compeyson was the man who abandoned Miss Havisham on their wedding day.

WHY ARE THESE CHAPTERS IMPORTANT?

A We learn about **Magwitch's past** for the first time.

B Pip's life has been taken in an **unexpected new direction**.

KEY THEME: SOCIAL CLASS (A03)

In these chapters we learn about Magwitch's background and life of crime, mainly spent with the shadowy figure of Compeyson. Magwitch had a wretched childhood – he reveals 'I was a ragged little creetur' with no family to look after him, while Compeyson was 'set up fur a gentleman' (p. 338). You should be able to see the similarities in the low social status of Pip and Magwitch, and how they are both drawn to people of a higher social class. Compeyson's social class meant that he could persuade the judge that he deserved a lighter prison sentence, whereas Magwitch was punished harshly. Victorian society was very class conscious and Dickens wrote about the poor and the victimised throughout his books. He was angered by the way that Victorian society was so unfair to people from a low social background. Pip continually feels guilty about his ambition to be a gentleman because of the way it takes him away from the kindly, but lower-class Joe and his humble working-class background at the forge.

KEY QUOTATION: PIP'S HORROR OF MAGWITCH (A02)

It is important to remember that Magwitch is full of pride and love for Pip and he is immensely pleased that he has managed to make Pip into a gentleman. Pip, however, is horrified by the real identity of his benefactor. This plot detail helps Dickens to create an unspoken tension during these chapters. Pip says, 'he [Magwitch] had no perception of the possibility of my finding any fault with my good fortune' (p. 332). The opposing views of the situation create a huge gap between the two characters. This gap is gradually closed, as Pip learns to appreciate Magwitch's good intentions and kindness, making Magwitch's death scene (in Chapter 56), where Dickens describes Pip holding Magwitch's hand, so much more memorable.

TOP TIP (A02)

Notice how Dickens is beginning to bring strands of the plot together: the convicts, Satis House and the 'expectations'.

KEY CONTEXT (A03)

The Victorian world that Dickens portrays is a mixture of wealthy aristocracy (Drummle, Compeyson and Miss Havisham), the rich middle classes (Pumblechook, Jaggers and the Pockets), the working classes (Joe, Trabb and Wemmick) and the criminal and destitute (Molly and Magwitch). Dickens was fascinated by the tensions created when these classes collide, for example, the connections between Compeyson and Magwitch or Pip and Drummle.

CHAPTERS 43–5: ESTELLA IS TO BE MARRIED

SUMMARY

- Pip feels that he must see Estella and Miss Havisham one last time before he leaves the country with Magwitch. When he goes to Richmond he finds that Estella has gone to Miss Havisham's so he follows her.
- At the Blue Boar he finds Bentley Drummle announcing that he is to dine with a young lady that evening. Pip sees a man in the inn yard who reminds him of Orlick.
- Pip confronts Miss Havisham about his mistaken beliefs and she admits she was wrong. She will help him support Herbert's career.
- Pip tells Estella he loves her and has always believed that they were meant for each other. Estella tells Pip that she is to marry Drummle.
- With Estella's announcement Pip's dreams are shattered and he is so upset that he walks all the way back to London. When he arrives at the gate of the Temple he is given a note from Wemmick telling him not to go home. Pip spends the night in a hotel but cannot sleep.
- Pip goes to see Wemmick at Walworth. Wemmick tells him he heard some prison gossip about Magwitch's return from Australia and also that someone has been watching Pip and his benefactor.
- Pip also finds out from Wemmick that Compeyson is in London. Wemmick has informed Herbert of the danger and Herbert has arranged lodgings for Magwitch at the house near the river where his girlfriend Clara lives with her father. This will be convenient for secretly getting on board a ship when the time comes.

WHY ARE THESE CHAPTERS IMPORTANT?

A   Pip finally forces Miss Havisham to **admit** she was not his benefactor and she has deceived him by allowing him to believe that.

B   Pip is faced with his greatest **dread**: Estella is to marry Drummle.

C   Pip is in **danger** because of Magwitch's **illegal presence** in London.

KEY CHARACTER: BENTLEY DRUMMLE   (A02)

Bentley Drummle is given no sympathetic characteristics at all and is a typical Dickensian villain, alongside Orlick in *Great Expectations*, but also Sykes in *Oliver Twist* and Wackford Squeers in *Nicholas Nickleby*. Like these **characters**, he is a cruel and violent bully. Such characters in **novels** can provide interesting tension and plot developments for the **protagonists** to battle against. Drummle is an example of how being of a higher social class does not automatically make you a gentleman. However, Dickens can even find humour in scenes with Drummle, such as when Drummle and Pip tussle for the best place in front of the fire, with Pip commenting, 'I was wondering who it was who kept the fire off' (p. 346).

CHECKPOINT 31 (A02)

What change does Pip now see in Miss Havisham?

TOP TIP (A01)

It is important to bear in mind that Estella has much in common with Pip: she is an orphan whose childhood experiences of cruelty and fear form the adult she grows into. Pip, however, has the gentle influences of Joe, Herbert and Wemmick, whereas Estella is not just beautiful as the star in her name, but also cold and distant right until the end of the novel. She is as tragic and damaged as Miss Havisham in many ways.

KEY CONTEXT (A03)

Consider reading some of Dickens's other novels that present young men facing difficulties, such as *David Copperfield* (1850) or *Oliver Twist* (1838).

EXAM FOCUS: WRITING ABOUT THEMES SUCH AS LOVE (A01)

You may be asked to write about a particular theme in depth and the most successful answers demonstrate an ability to understand the theme across the novel and in particular chapters. The following is a successful response to a question about how Dickens develops the theme of love:

> In Chapter 44, Dickens presents Estella and Pip describing their experience of love. Pip's language is simple and honest: 'I have loved you ever since I first saw you in this house' (p. 353). Despite this, Estella does not appear to display any emotions. Dickens describes her as being 'unmoved' twice on the same page despite Pip's 'miserable' appearance (p. 353). Estella says to Pip 'When you say you love me, I know what you mean, as a form of words ... you touch nothing there' (p. 353), which echoes the way that Miss Havisham speaks throughout the novel, such as in the first visit to Miss Havisham where she instructs Estella to 'break his heart' (Chapter 8, p. 57). It is only with the minor characters in the novel that the theme of love is presented in a more simple way, such as Herbert and Wemmick. Love for Pip, Estella and Miss Havisham leads to pain and misery.

Refers to Dickens explicitly as the author

Refers to detail across the text relevant to theme

Uses appropriate technical vocabulary

Now you try it:

Find another scene where love is presented – perhaps a scene with Wemmick and his father – and select two or three details that demonstrate how Dickens is presenting this theme. Start:
It is clear that Wemmick has a great deal of affection for his father...

TOP TIP (A01)

Planning your answer in the exam means you should be able to put your thoughts into a structured order: this will help you demonstrate you can write in a critical style.

CHAPTERS 46–8: ESTELLA'S MOTHER AND PLANS FOR MAGWITCH

SUMMARY

- Pip visits Magwitch who is lodging with Mrs Whimple by the river. He is introduced to Clara who looks after her bedridden father. Pip tells Magwitch of Wemmick's plans to help him escape, but says nothing about Compeyson in case Magwitch is tempted to go after him. Pip feels a genuine concern for Magwitch.
- Magwitch agrees to Pip's idea that they should leave the country and is pleased when Herbert suggests that Pip should buy a boat. Magwitch and Herbert become familiar sights on the river.
- Pip cannot get rid of the feeling he is being watched nor forget his fears for the safety of Magwitch. Pip awaits more news from Wemmick.
- One evening Pip goes to see Mr Wopsle in a play. During the performance Pip notices the actor staring at him. After the play Wopsle tells him he was staring at the man behind Pip. Pip realises it was Compeyson.
- Pip dines at Jaggers's home once again and realises that the mysterious maid, Molly, is Estella's mother. Wemmick later tells him that Jaggers had defended Molly twenty years earlier on a charge of strangling a woman and that she was said to have murdered her own three-year-old daughter.

WHY ARE THESE CHAPTERS IMPORTANT?

- **A** The **plotlines** involving Magwitch, Compeyson, Miss Havisham and Estella are coming together.
- **B** Pip finds out that Molly is Estella's **mother**.
- **C** Pip is living in a constant state of **anxiety**.

KEY LANGUAGE: FORMS OF ADDRESS (A01)

Victorian society had many rules about the ways that people could address each other that we might find surprising today. Pip always addresses Jaggers as 'Mr Jaggers' because he sees Jaggers as superior to him, whereas Jaggers just calls him 'Pip'. Earlier in the novel Pip is annoyed by Joe calling him 'Mr Pip' and 'Sir' because he doesn't want Joe to act as if Pip is above him. Jaggers calls Bentley Drummle 'the Spider' almost as a term of affection. Jaggers calls Wemmick 'Wemmick': he does not need to use 'Mr' because he is Wemmick's boss and in a position of power. Servants are the lowest of the social ladder: when Jaggers says 'Molly, Molly, Molly, Molly, how slow you are to-day!' (p. 381) he is not only showing his control over this physically powerful woman, but is also using a typical form of address for a servant in a Victorian household.

> **TOP TIP** (A02)
>
> Notice how Dickens hints at further developments in the plot in order to build up suspense.

> **TOP TIP** (A04)
>
> Make sure you know the nicknames for characters such as Provis/Magwitch and Handel/Pip and you have learnt the correct spelling.

KEY QUOTATION: PIP'S RELATIONSHIP WITH MAGWITCH **A02**

Pip's natural kindness and compassion for Magwitch continue to be revealed, despite his anxiety about helping an escaped criminal. When Pip leaves Magwitch, he says: 'I little supposed my heart could ever be as heavy and anxious at parting from him as it was now' (p. 370). This is echoed by Pip's kindness towards Estella, Miss Havisham and even Mrs Joe, despite the cruelty they inflict on him. However, Pip is not overly soft or forgiving: he cannot forgive Orlick, Drummle or Compeyson for the way they hurt both him and the people around him.

TOP TIP: WRITING ABOUT DICKENS'S USE OF SYMBOLISM **A02**

Dickens often adds symbolic details to the places where his characters live, work and visit that help us understand something about the stories and themes. This is most obvious in Satis House, for example, where Miss Havisham's misery and illness are symbolised by the mouldy wedding feast and closed curtains. However, the best exam answers show understanding of more than just one setting in the novel. Jaggers's office at the law courts has some equally interesting details, such as the two plaster casts of the hanged criminals which flicker in the candlelight making Pip feel they are playing 'a diabolical game at bo-peep with me' and the 'winding-sheets' that remind Pip of the 'hanged clients' (p. 380). The details of this office may symbolise Jaggers's involvement with the dark side of the justice system: hangings, misery and fear. Look at the details that Dickens provides about other settings, such as the Pockets' home, the city of London itself, the forge, Wemmick's house and so on and note down what they might be conveying to the reader.

CHECKPOINT 32 A01

Why is it important that Dickens tells us that Pip feels he is being watched?

CHAPTERS 49–52: FIRE AT SATIS HOUSE AND THE TRUTH ABOUT ESTELLA

SUMMARY

- Pip goes to see Miss Havisham, finding her full of remorse. She signs a note for Jaggers to release money for Herbert. Pip forgives her for her cruelty and deception.
- Pip learns that Estella is now married to Drummle. Miss Havisham does not know anything about Estella's parents, only that Jaggers brought her to Satis House when she was two or three years old.
- Pip is about to leave Satis House for possibly the last time, but he imagines he sees Miss Havisham hanging from a beam. Terrified, he runs to her room.

- Miss Havisham is there, but suddenly her clothes catch fire. She will die from her injuries. Pip receives burns to his hands and arms. As he leaves, Miss Havisham is still regretting the harm she has done.
- Back in London, Herbert looks after Pip. Herbert says Magwitch told him how a woman he was involved with had been charged with murder and had threatened to kill their child. Pip realises he has been talking about Estella's mother. Magwitch believes that the woman carried out her threat. Pip tells Herbert that he is sure that Magwitch is Estella's father.
- Pip tells Jaggers about the fire and Miss Havisham's injuries and that he knows who Estella's mother and father are. Jaggers admits that he took in the murderess as his housekeeper and gave up her daughter for adoption, but recommends that Pip remains quiet.
- Pip receives a letter from Wemmick suggesting he makes a move in the next few days. Herbert and Pip decide to wait for a steamer bound for Hamburg in a quiet place down river and then row out to it so that Pip and Magwitch can get on board. They arrange to pick up Magwitch from his lodgings on Wednesday.
- Pip is sent an anonymous letter inviting him to the marshes alone to receive information about Magwitch. Pip rushes to the marshes, lying to Herbert about where he is going. He has a sense there is danger ahead but goes anyway.

CHECKPOINT 33 (A02)

What might the reader make of Pip's behaviour here?

TOP TIP (A01)

Remember there is a kinder side to Jaggers. After the truth is disclosed about Magwitch and the identity of Estella's parents, he reveals a more human side to his **character**. Jaggers gave up Estella for adoption because he felt moved to save at least one child from the fate of so many he had seen pass through the legal system.

WHY ARE THESE CHAPTERS IMPORTANT?

A   These are the **final scenes** between Pip and Miss Havisham.

B   Estella's **parentage** is finally confirmed.

C   The final **plots** involving Magwitch and Orlick are set in place.

AIMING HIGH: THE FIRE AT SATIS HOUSE

This scene is the final chapter in Miss Havisham's tragic story and is the last chance for Pip to receive answers to questions about Estella as well as for him to open his heart to Miss Havisham. Estella's violent and abusive marriage to Drummle has not been the 'revenge' on men that Miss Havisham has intended and has brought a 'new desolation' (p. 390) to the house. Miss Havisham cries 'What have I done!' (p. 390) repeatedly to show her regret. We see more evidence of Pip's great kindness and compassion in the face of Miss Havisham's 'master mania' (p. 390) as he calls it. Dickens ironically makes the environment that Miss Havisham has built around herself the cause of her own death, as the dry and brittle wedding dress catches fire accidentally. Earlier in the novel Miss Havisham predicts she will be laid out on the dining table when she has died and this is what happens. This eerie prediction along with the 'black shower' of tinder and the 'disturbed beetles and spiders' (p. 393) is a suitably Gothic ending to Miss Havisham's story.

CHECKPOINT 34 **A02**

What does Miss Havisham realise at the end of her life?

CHAPTERS 53–5: ORLICK ATTACKS PIP, MAGWITCH IS CAPTURED

SUMMARY

- Pip knows the marshes well and finds the sluice-house where he has been told to wait. He is attacked from behind, tied to a ladder against the wall and is in great pain because of his burns.

- Pip discovers it is Orlick. He has been working with Compeyson and says that Magwitch will be captured.

- Orlick is about to kill Pip with a hammer when the door bursts open and Pip is saved by Herbert.

- Back in London, Pip, Herbert and Startop take their boat from the Temple stairs and start rowing down river with Magwitch disguised as a river pilot. Pip is uneasy and sees two men looking at their boat during the night.

- As the steamer approaches they are hailed from another rowing boat and Magwitch is called upon to surrender. Magwitch shows that Compeyson is in the boat with the police. At that moment they are run down by the steamer.

CHECKPOINT 35 (AO3)

How does Orlick feel about Biddy?

- Magwitch is later pulled from the river and manacled. He is badly injured. Compeyson drowns.

- Magwitch's trial for returning from transportation is set for a month's time. Pip shows strong loyalty towards Magwitch.

- Herbert announces that he will soon be leaving to run his firm's branch in Cairo. He offers Pip a job as clerk with the prospects of promotion to partner.

- Wemmick marries Miss Skiffins and Pip is enrolled as the best man. The comic scene at the Walworth wedding provides a humorous contrast to the sad events in London.

WHY ARE THESE CHAPTERS IMPORTANT?

A The final scenes between Orlick and Pip are shockingly **violent**.

B Magwitch's escape attempt fails, much to Pip's **devastation**.

C Compeyson – the cause of so much **misery** – finally loses his life.

KEY THEME: PHYSICAL VIOLENCE (A02)

There is a great deal of violence and action throughout *Great Expectations*. The fight here between Orlick and Pip shows Pip in genuine danger of losing his life. This level of physical threat can be seen throughout the **novel**, from Magwitch's threats towards the young Pip, the fight between Joe and Orlick, Mrs Joe's aggression and Bentley Drummle's abusive behaviour towards Estella. Death or serious injury was a constant presence in Victorian life, when hospitals, health and safety laws and policing were all in their infancy.

> **CHECKPOINT 36 (A02)**
>
> How does Pip reveal the good side of his nature in the episode on the river?

REVISION FOCUS: ORLICK

Orlick is sometimes described as a 'malcontent'. This is the name for a literary **character** who exists to cause misery for others. Make a note of Orlick's appearances in the novel, and the effect he has on the plot and characters.

CHAPTERS 56–9: MAGWITCH DIES, THE FINAL MEETING WITH ESTELLA

SUMMARY

- Pip visits Magwitch in the prison infirmary every day and sees him grow weaker. When Magwitch comes to trial he is sentenced to death.

- Pip continues to visit Magwitch and the convict's health steadily deteriorates. Pip tells him that his daughter (Estella) is a beautiful lady. Magwitch kisses Pip's hand and dies.

- Pip falls ill and is almost arrested for debt. When he recovers he finds that Joe has been looking after him. When Pip enquires about Miss Havisham, Joe tells him that she has died. Most of her estate has been left to Estella.

- Pip gradually recovers. Joe pays off his debt. Pip has also decided to ask Biddy to marry him and he assumes that Biddy will accept his proposal. However, not long afterwards Joe and Biddy marry. Pip is thankful that he never mentioned to Joe his own thoughts of marrying Biddy.

- Pip leaves the country and goes to work for Herbert to pay off his debts. Eleven years later he returns to visit Joe and Biddy at the forge; they have a little boy whom they have named after him.

- Pip walks to Satis House and is surprised to meet Estella, who is now a widow after the violent death of Bentley Drummle. This is the first time Estella has been back. She hopes they can still be friends even though they will be apart. Pip takes her hand and as they leave the garden he appears to believe that they will always be together, despite Estella's ambiguous comments.

TOP TIP (A01)

Remember to look at the way Joe embodies the values that Pip takes the whole novel to appreciate: honesty, kindness and hard work are more important than being rich or popular. Joe is not a feeble character, however; his physical and moral strength are clear when he confronts Mrs Joe and Orlick.

WHY ARE THESE CHAPTERS IMPORTANT?

A **Magwitch dies** with the comfort of knowing something of his lost daughter, Estella.

B Pip is able to put his mistakes behind him through **hard work** abroad.

C Pip **appears** to be reunited with Estella.

KEY CONTEXT: THE JUSTICE SYSTEM (A03)

CHECKPOINT 37 (A03)

Magwitch is too weak to stand as he is sentenced to death. What does this tell you about British justice at that time?

Dickens began his writing career as a court reporter and saw for himself the way that prisoners and defendants were treated. When Magwitch comes to trial, Pip is allowed to stand near the dock and hold his hand but the trial is a mere formality as it is obvious that Magwitch has committed the crime of returning to England from Australia. Magwitch is sentenced to death with thirty-one other prisoners on the last day of the Court Sessions. The mass sentence of death on thirty-two prisoners is a reminder of the inhumanity of the legal system at that time. Dickens makes references to hangings, prison hulks, chains and manacles and so on throughout the novel.

KEY THEME: REDEMPTION A02

Redemption means making up for past faults and finding peace and forgiveness. The ending of *Great Expectations* gives redemption for Pip. He works hard abroad to pay off his debts and become an honest, hardworking man. Before this, he writes appeals and petitions to the Home Secretary and other important people on Magwitch's behalf showing great devotion to Magwitch in his final days. It redeems him in our eyes because he can gain no credit in polite society for being associated with a convict. When he realises that Magwitch is about to die he tells him that his daughter 'is a lady and very beautiful. And I love her!' (p. 451) which comforts Magwitch greatly. Magwitch kisses Pip's hand before he dies – the final stage in his development as a sensitive and vulnerable human being.

KEY CONTEXT A03

Magwitch's deathbed scene is typical of Victorian fiction and has been described as 'sentimental', which means it is deliberately emotional.

AIMING HIGH: EVALUATING THE ENDING OF *GREAT EXPECTATIONS*

Successful responses to exam questions explore the text and put forward different arguments about its features rather than just describing main events and characters. The ending of *Great Expectations* has been described as 'romantic' because it reunites Pip and Estella, but it is important that you can see this is actually quite a problematic ending for the following reasons:

- Estella has been brought up to hate men. She knows no other way to behave and it seems unrealistic that she can change, even after eleven years.

- Pip's romantic ideals relate to the young Estella that he first met at Satis House when he was a boy. He does not know anything of the adult and worldly Estella.

This may be why the final line of the novel, 'I saw no shadow of another parting from her' (p. 475), is deliberately ambiguous – it has more than one possible meaning. It could actually mean that there is a parting hanging over them like a 'shadow', but that Pip just could not see it. This interpretation is strengthened by Estella saying that they will 'continue friends apart' (p. 475).

KEY CONTEXT A03

Dickens did not want the happy ending between Pip and Estella. He only used it because friends advised him that the original ending (in which they part) was too sad.

PROGRESS AND REVISION CHECK

SECTION ONE: CHECK YOUR KNOWLEDGE

Answer these quick questions to test your basic knowledge of the **novel**, its **characters** and events:

1. What profession does Pip's uncle Joe Gargery have?
2. Who demands Pip brings him 'wittles' (p. 3)?
3. What were the prison hulks?
4. Who is the young girl who lives with Miss Havisham?
5. Who takes Pip as an apprentice in Chapter 14?
6. What object is found next to Mrs Joe after she is attacked in Chapter 16?
7. In Chapter 22, Pip meets Herbert Pocket for the second time. When did Pip first meet Herbert?
8. Who is nicknamed 'the Spider' by Jaggers?
9. How much money does Jaggers give to Pip from his benefactor on Pip's twenty-first birthday?
10. Who goes by the name of Provis?
11. Pip accuses Miss Havisham of deliberately misleading him. What does he mistakenly believe about Miss Havisham?
12. When walking through the gardens of Satis House in Chapter 49, what ghostly vision does Pip have?
13. Who gave Estella to Miss Havisham for adoption on behalf of Molly, Estella's birth mother?
14. Who ties Pip to a ladder in Chapter 53?
15. What sentence is handed out to Magwitch after he is caught by the guards trying to escape in Chapter 56?
16. Who holds Magwitch's hand as he dies?
17. Orlick eventually ends up in prison for robbery, but who is it he attempted to rob?
18. What do Joe and Biddy call their son?
19. How is Bentley Drummle killed?
20. In whose firm does Pip become a partner?

PROGRESS AND REVISION CHECK

SECTION TWO: CHECK YOUR UNDERSTANDING

Here are two tasks about the significance of particular moments in the novel. These require more thought and slightly longer responses. In each case, try to write at least three to four paragraphs.

Task 1: Look at the section in which Pip arrives in London in Chapter 20. What impressions does Pip have of the new setting in which he has arrived? Think about:

- the language that Dickens uses to describe London
- how Pip responds to his new environment

Task 2: In Chapter 53, Orlick nearly kills Pip. What does this chapter tell us about Orlick's relationship with Pip? Think about:

- the language Dickens uses to describe Orlick

PROGRESS CHECK

GOOD PROGRESS

I can:

- Understand how Dickens has sequenced and revealed events. ☐
- Refer to the importance of key events in the novel. ☐
- Select well-chosen evidence, including key quotations, to support my ideas. ☐

EXCELLENT PROGRESS

I can:

- Refer in depth to main and minor events and how they contribute to the development of the plot. ☐
- Understand how Dickens has carefully ordered or revealed events for particular effects. ☐
- Draw on a range of carefully selected key evidence, including quotations, to support my ideas. ☐

WHO'S WHO?

PIP

PIP'S ROLE IN THE NOVEL

Pip is an orphan who is brought up by his sister at a blacksmith's forge in the Kent marshes. During the **novel** he:

- meets an escaped convict as a child, and brings him food and a file.
- is invited to play at the house of a rich but strange woman called Miss Havisham.
- meets the love of his life, Estella, who is Miss Havisham's adopted daughter.
- is apprenticed as blacksmith, but leaves for London when he receives money from a mysterious benefactor.
- attempts to become a gentleman in London but quickly falls into debt.
- finds out that his benefactor is Magwitch, the escaped convict from his childhood.
- has to stand by as Estella marries a violent bully.
- learns the true identity of Estella's parents.
- forgives Magwitch, Miss Havisham and Estella for their cruelty.
- finally learns that being a gentleman is about kindness, generosity and hard work.

PIP'S IMPORTANCE TO THE NOVEL AS A WHOLE

Pip is the central **protagonist** of the novel and is the **narrator**, which means we see all the events from Pip's point of view. Pip's search for his 'great expectations' allows Dickens to write about many aspects of Victorian society through Pip's experience of childhood, city and country life, riches and poverty, love and loss.

CHECKPOINT 38

What game does Pip first try to play at Miss Havisham's?

EXAM FOCUS: WRITING ABOUT PIP

Key point	Evidence/Further meaning
At the start of the **novel**, Pip is an innocent boy who has been brought up to respect his elders and betters.	• Pip is kind and generous towards Magwitch because he has been taught not to be selfish. On giving Magwitch his food, the young Pip comments, 'I am glad you enjoy it' (Ch. 3, p. 17). • Pip tolerates Miss Havisham's cruelty even as an adult because of his naturally respectful manner. • Pip is surrounded by **characters** such as Mr Pumblechook and Jaggers who treat him with rudeness and contempt.
As a gentleman, he is quick to drop the people who have been his friends and family in case they embarrass him.	• Once Pip has come into his money, he is embarrassed by Joe Gargery and avoids seeing him. • Pip learns that being a gentleman is not just about the amount of money that you have: meeting rich but unpleasant people like Bentley Drummle help him to understand this. • Biddy hints with 'sweet tack and kindness' (Ch. 57, p. 460) that Pip is being unfair to people such as Joe.
By helping Magwitch, Pip demonstrates selflessness and compassion.	• Pip doesn't just bring Magwitch food because he is frightened: the reader senses that he genuinely wants to help him. • Pip is at first horrified by Magwitch's return because it means his money has come from his 'convict on the marshes' (Ch. 39, p. 316). • Pip learns to appreciate Magwitch's kindness and eventually risks his own freedom to help Magwitch.
Pip's obsessive love for Estella continues until the end of the novel.	• Pip confesses to Biddy, 'I admire her dreadfully, and I want to be a gentleman on her account' (Ch. 17, p. 125). • Estella's marriage to Bentley Drummle devastates Pip. • Pip clearly wants to stay with Estella, but in the final chapter she says they will be 'friends apart'.

TOP TIP: THE CHARACTERS IN PIP'S LIFE

Make sure you can see how all the different characters have varied roles in Pip's life, often providing contrasts and similarities. Pip's biological father is dead, but Joe (Chapters 2–4, 7, 14–15, 27, 57, 59), Jaggers (Chapters 20, 28, 40, 51), Magwitch (Chapters 1, 39, 51, 52, 56) and Wemmick (Chapters 21, 25) all provide types of parental roles for him. Pip's contemporaries also help us to see different sides of his character: the contrast with characters such as Orlick and Drummle helps us see Pip's gentleness, whereas Herbert provides a much better role model for Pip as a gentleman. Ultimately, Pip's growth and development form the heart of the novel.

CHECKPOINT 39 A02

Where does Pip imagine he sees Miss Havisham hanging?

JOE

JOE'S ROLE IN THE NOVEL

Joe is a simple, honest blacksmith who has married Pip's sister. He acts as Pip's companion during the boy's early years. Joe's clear, basic values make him stand out from the more dishonest characters in the novel. Joe:

- loves Pip but never tries to stand in the boy's way, even when Pip is rude and snobbish about Joe's humble background at the forge.
- cares for the adult Pip when he is ill but he knows that there is a gap between them which can never be fully closed since Pip has become a gentleman.
- has a simple dignity and knows that he is seen at his best in his place of work. This teaches Pip about the value of work.
- will be a good husband to Biddy and a father to little Pip. He deserves the happiness he has found and which Pip envies, but does not begrudge him.

EXAM FOCUS: WRITING ABOUT JOE

Key point	Evidence/Further meaning
Dickens explores the importance of literacy and learning to read through the character of Joe.	• Joe was unable to learn to read because of his violent father, a 'drawback on [his] learning' (Ch. 7, p. 44). • By the end of the novel Biddy has taught Joe to read and he can write a note for Pip.
Joe can be strong and determined even though he appears to be badly treated by Mrs Joe.	• Pip describes Joe as a 'Hercules in strength' (Ch. 2, p. 6). • Joe and Orlick fight in Chapter 15, with Dickens describing them as 'two giants' (p. 111).
His love for Pip is unconditional despite Pip's snobbish behaviour towards him.	• Joe says to Pip, 'Ever the best of friends; ain't us, Pip?', but Pip is 'ashamed to answer him' (Ch. 57, p. 459). • Pip feels irritated when Joe calls him 'Sir' (Ch. 57, p. 461). • Joe shows his love for Pip when he calls his own son 'Pip'.
Dickens always represents Joe's rural accent and **dialect** through his spelling.	• Joe says 'your elth's your elth' (Ch. 2, p. 9), typically not pronouncing his aitches. • Joe says to Pip, 'God knows as I forgive you, if I have anythink to forgive!' (Ch. 58, p. 471).

MISS HAVISHAM

MISS HAVISHAM'S ROLE IN THE NOVEL

Miss Havisham lives in a former brewery called Satis House. In the **novel**, she:

- wants to take revenge on all men for the wrong that was done by her fiancé, Compeyson, who jilted her just before their marriage.
- sits in the clothes she wore for her wedding and is surrounded by decaying things in a darkened room.
- adopts a young girl, Estella, whom she plans to use to take her revenge on all men.
- delights in the way that Estella torments Pip and likes to keep her relatives guessing as to whom she will leave her money.
- allows Pip to believe that she is his mysterious benefactor.
- has a terrible impact on Pip and Estella.
- tries to undo some of the harm she has done by helping Pip with his plan for Herbert and leaves her cousin Matthew a legacy.
- is distraught with guilt for what she has done to Estella and to Pip at the end of her life, although Pip forgives her.
- dies when her ruined wedding dress catches fire.

EXAM FOCUS: WRITING ABOUT MISS HAVISHAM

Key point	Evidence/Further meaning
Miss Havisham has become mentally unstable before the start of the novel.	• Her confusion manifests itself by the state of Satis House: permanently closed windows and the left-over wedding feast full of beetles. • Pip says, 'the bride within the bridal dress had withered like the dress' (Ch. 8, p. 55).
She has almost no interaction with the outside world.	• She tells Pip, 'I know nothing of the days of the week' (Ch. 8, p. 59). • Miss Havisham never leaves Satis House.
She brings up Estella to break men's hearts	• This is why she forces Pip and Estella to play together as children. • Estella cannot make normal friendships because of her upbringing. • As an adult, Estella says, 'I am what you have made me' (Ch. 38, p. 298).
Miss Havisham eventually realises she treated Pip and Estella badly.	• Miss Havisham confesses to Pip, 'But as she grew, and promised to be very beautiful, I gradually did worse' (Ch. 49, p. 391). • Miss Havisham's last request to Pip is to write 'I forgive her', which he does (Ch. 49, p. 394).

ESTELLA

ESTELLA'S ROLE IN THE NOVEL

Estella is a beautiful young girl, brought up as a young lady by Miss Havisham. She uses her education to talk down to Pip and make him feel inferior. In the novel, she:

- does not fully realise, when she is a child, that she is being used by Miss Havisham as an agent for Miss Havisham's revenge.
- is educated as an accomplished and sophisticated young lady.
- warns Pip that she has no heart and can never love anyone.
- tells Pip that he is the only one she can be honest with and that she makes fools of all the other men.
- never finds out that her mother is Molly and her father is Magwitch.
- is self-destructive in her determination to marry the brutal Bentley Drummle – even Miss Havisham tries to dissuade her.
- is a young widow at the end of the novel and has little property left.
- appears softened by her experiences, and implies that she regrets having rejected Pip's love for her but feels that the best she can hope for is that they are friends.

EXAM FOCUS: WRITING ABOUT ESTELLA (A01)

Key point	Evidence/Further meaning
Estella's **character** is cruel and cold right from her childhood.	• We first see Estella in the role of gatekeeper, shutting Pumblechook out as she lets Pip into Satis House. • Estella repeatedly calls Pip 'boy' (Ch. 8, p. 53) even though she is not much older than him. Pip says she is 'scornful' of him (p. 54).
Her beauty bewitches Pip.	• The name Estella means 'star'. • Pip quickly tells Miss Havisham that Estella is 'very pretty' (Ch. 8, p. 58).
She always tells Pip that he is the only person with whom she is honest.	• When Pip argues with Estella about flirting with Drummle, she says she will 'deceive and entrap' others – 'all of them but you' (Ch. 38, p. 305). • She tells Pip that she will not be 'a blessing' to Drummle (Ch. 44, p. 355). • Even at the conclusion of the novel, Estella cannot pretend that all will be well between her and Pip.
Estella's cold nature has been created by Miss Havisham.	• Estella tells Pip that when he says he loves her, she understands that 'as a form of words' (Ch. 44, p. 353) and cannot understand the emotion. • When Miss Havisham tells Estella it is not in her nature to marry Drummle, Estella says, 'It is in the nature formed within me' (Ch. 44, p. 354). She makes it clear to Miss Havisham that this marriage results from Estella's own misery and loneliness.

ABEL MAGWITCH

MAGWITCH'S ROLE IN THE NOVEL

We first meet Magwitch at the start of the **novel** when he escapes from the prison hulks and asks Pip to bring him food and a file. At first, like Pip, we are repelled by Magwitch's coarse appearance and rough habits but as we learn of his brutal life we become more sympathetic towards him. In the novel, he:

- is transported to Australia as a punishment for his crimes.
- makes his fortune in Australia, which he sends to Pip via Jaggers, allowing Pip to come to London and become a gentleman.
- is revealed as a partner in crime with Compeyson, the man who abandoned Miss Havisham.
- is revealed to be the father of Estella.
- has pride in the gentleman he has created in Pip and they form a strong affection for each other.
- feels that Pip is a replacement for the child he lost.
- is told as he is dying that his daughter, Estella, is alive and is a beautiful lady.

EXAM FOCUS: WRITING ABOUT MAGWITCH

Key point	Evidence/Further meaning
Magwitch is yet another **character** who has a troubled childhood.	• Magwitch tells Pip he doesn't know where he was born and never knew his parents. • His earliest memory is stealing turnips to survive. • He describes himself as 'hardened' as a child (Ch. 42, p. 338).
He plays an essential role in making Pip a gentleman.	• Magwitch tells Pip, 'I'm your second father. You're my son – more to me nor any son' (Ch. 39, p. 313). • Both Pip and Magwitch assume that obtaining money is the route to becoming a gentleman, but Pip learns that this is not true.
He is described as dramatically ugly and frightening.	• The descriptions of Magwitch at the start of the novel make references to grotesque violence such as cannibalism. • When Magwitch touches the adult Pip, Pip says 'I shuddered at the thought that … his hand might be stained with blood' (Ch. 39, p. 315).
Magwitch's death is surprisingly moving.	• By the time Magwitch is dying in prison, Pip has learnt to feel love and compassion for him and visits every day. • As he approaches death Magwitch is described as looking at Pip 'affectionately', resting 'gently' and appearing 'placid' (Ch. 56, p. 451).

MR JAGGERS

JAGGERS'S ROLE IN THE NOVEL

Jaggers, a London lawyer, first appears in the novel when he meets Pip on the stairs of Satis House. In the novel, he:

- visits Pip some years later to tell him that he is to be wealthy.
- knows all along who Pip's mysterious benefactor really is, but never gives the secret away.
- organises Pip's tutoring and accommodation in London and introduces him to Bentley Drummle for the first time.
- also works for Miss Havisham and arranges her adoption of Estella.
- has a clerk called Wemmick who becomes a good friend to Pip.

CHECKPOINT 40 (A01)

Before his dinner party, Jaggers goes through an elaborate routine of washing (Ch. 26, p. 205). What does that suggest about his character?

EXAM FOCUS: WRITING ABOUT JAGGERS (A01)

Key point	Evidence/Further meaning
Jaggers is king in the world of criminal law.	- Even criminals are frightened of him: he doesn't need to lock his doors at home because he is held in 'dread' by local criminals (Ch. 25, p. 200). - Dickens describes him as 'highly dictatorial' (Ch. 51, p. 406).
He brings to life the dark and violent side of the Victorian criminal justice system.	- Jaggers's office contains two plaster casts of convicts that are 'odious' (Ch. 24, p. 194) and 'brutal' (Ch. 51, p. 400). - He 'tames' Molly, Estella's violent birth mother, and makes her his servant.
He inspires fear and awe in everyone around around him.	- Clients who wait to see him are full of anxiety. One even sings a strange song, 'Oh, Jaggerth, Jaggerth, Jaggerth!' (Ch. 20, p. 161). - He is not intimidated by Miss Havisham, Bentley Drummle or Mr Pumblechook, for example.
Jaggers has a human side that Dickens occasionally shows us.	- Jaggers 'start[s]' (Ch. 51, p. 401), meaning he jumps in surprise, when Pip tells him he knows who Magwitch is. - He hints he has had 'poor dreams' (Ch. 51, p. 403) of a pleasant home. - Jaggers says Pip would be wiser to chop off his hand with a 'cleaver' rather than put Estella through the humiliation of having her parentage public knowledge (Ch. 51, p. 405).

MINOR CHARACTERS

HERBERT

Herbert is a perfect gentleman. Although their first meeting as boys at Satis House ends in a fight, Pip remembers feeling 'but a gloomy satisfaction' at winning (Ch. 11, p. 89). Herbert is tactful and kind when teaching Pip table manners, dealing with a potentially embarrassing situation 'in such a lively way that [they] both laughed' (Ch. 22, p. 174). He is an honest friend to Pip, and a delightful companion and business colleague, with Pip admiring his 'cheerful industry and readiness' (Ch. 58, p. 471). Herbert supports Pip in his attempt to flee with Magwitch and saves his life at the sluice-house near the limekiln on the marshes. His refreshing take on Estella is that she is a 'tartar' and that he had a lucky escape not to be in Pip's position (Ch. 22, p. 171). At the end of the **novel** he is happily married to Clara and successful in his career.

MR WEMMICK

Wemmick provides some of the humour in the novel: as Jaggers's clerk he leads a double life as the whimsical architect and smallholder of Walworth. His home has pigs and rabbits and his cottage has a turret with the top decorated to look 'like a battery mounted with guns' (Ch. 25, p. 201). He is described as 'a dry man, rather short in stature, with a square wooden face' (Ch. 21, p. 165). Much of Wemmick's private life is devoted to looking after and entertaining 'the Aged', his very old, deaf, but 'clean, cheerful, comfortable' father (Ch. 25, p. 202). In London he is well known as Jaggers's man and acts as an intermediary between Jaggers and his criminal clients. He shows great kindness towards Pip but likes to confine any personal business to Walworth. His motto is 'Get hold of portable property' (Ch. 24, p. 196).

BENTLEY DRUMMLE

Drummle is a fellow student at Matthew Pocket's whom Pip first meets in Chapter 23 not long after his arrival in London. Mrs Pocket is distracted by Drummle's being 'the next heir but one to a baronetcy' (Ch. 23, p. 186) and Drummle's aristocratic background allows him to behave rudely to people around him. He shows himself to be surly, bad-tempered and unsociable. He is arrogant and a bully, with Pip saying he has a 'blockhead confidence in his money and in his family greatness' (Ch. 38, p. 303). Drummle is a rival for Estella's affections and he finally persuades her to marry him. After treating Estella very badly – he is said to have 'used her with great cruelty' (Ch. 59, p. 473) – he dies in a riding accident involving a horse he has beaten.

ORLICK

As Joe's assistant at the forge, Orlick is bitterly resentful of Pip once Pip becomes the official apprentice. He has a hot temper and it is only Joe's superior strength that keeps him in check. He is described as 'morose' and 'slouching' and once told the young Pip that the Devil lived in the forge, just to frighten him (Ch. 15, p. 109).

Orlick's sinister presence makes itself felt throughout the story. He resents Pip as he thinks Pip has stopped Biddy from liking him and has caused him to lose his job at Miss Havisham's. Orlick is in league with Compeyson and helps him in his plot against Magwitch. He finally imprisons and nearly murders Pip. He confesses to the attack on Pip's sister, although he blames Pip for driving him to it, saying 'it warn't Old Orlick as did it; it was you' (Ch. 53, p. 417). He escapes when Pip is rescued. The last we hear of him is that he is in jail for robbing Pumblechook.

BIDDY

Biddy is an intelligent woman who works with the Gargerys at the forge. Pip describes her as 'extraordinary' (Ch. 17, p. 122) in her knowledge of the forge and her capable manner, and she becomes the local schoolteacher. She is 'pleasant and wholesome and sweet-tempered' (Ch. 17, p. 122). She sees that Pip's ambition will bring him a good deal of heartache and tells him so in Chapter 17. Biddy becomes Joe's housekeeper and eventually marries him. She resents the way that Pip neglects Joe, and frequently acts as Pip's conscience. Pip eventually admits to Biddy and Joe that he was 'ungenerous and unjust' in his treatment of them both and that he grew to see how they were so 'good and true' (Ch. 58, p. 470). In the early stage of the novel Biddy might well be in love with Pip but by the end she is described as 'matronly' and a contented wife and mother (Ch. 59, p. 472).

MR PUMBLECHOOK

A moderately successful corn-chandler who visits the forge to see Mrs Joe in particular, Pumblechook is actually Joe's uncle. Mrs Joe thinks it is very prestigious to have him at the house so she provides 'extensive arrangements' for their meals (Ch. 4, p. 20). He is described as having a 'mouth like a fish, dull staring eyes, and sandy hair standing upright' (Ch. 4, p. 22). Pip says he is 'wretched company' (Ch. 8, p. 51), who has the annoying habit of firing mathematical problems at Pip – 'Seven times nine, boy!' (Ch. 8, p. 52). Pumblechook is generally rude, pompous and opinionated. He delivers the message that Pip is to play at Miss Havisham's: he thereafter becomes a local legend as the man who made Pip's fortune, although Estella firmly shuts the gate in his face as he arrives at Satis House (Ch. 8, p. 52).

KEY CONTEXT (A03)

A corn-chandler makes money from buying and selling corn.

CHECKPOINT 41 (A02)

How does Pip manage to show Pumblechook's stupidity after the visit to Satis House?

MR WOPSLE

As the church clerk, Wopsle visits the Gargerys on the Christmas day when Pip encounters Magwitch. He is forever boasting that he would deliver better sermons than the vicar: Wopsle has 'a deep voice which he was uncommonly proud of' (Ch. 4, p. 21). Thwarted in his ambition to become a clergyman he takes to the stage in London where he enjoys mixed success. Wopsle also provides a moment of great anxiety in Chapter 47 ('Mr Wopsle's News') when he sees Compeyson sitting behind Pip in the theatre. His greatest claim to fame is his version of *Hamlet* which is greeted with jeers by the audience. Dickens was an actor and playwright himself and so would have encountered many such actors on the Victorian stages.

MRS JOE

Pip's elder sister, Mrs Joe is married to Joe Gargery and has brought Pip up 'by hand' which has the dual meaning of 'by herself' and 'with smacks' (Ch. 2, p. 5). She is scornful of Joe, calling him a 'dunder-headed king of the noodles' (Ch. 15, p. 110). She feels hard-done-by and both Pip and Joe are victims of her violent temper. She listens only to her relative Pumblechook, the corn-chandler. After she is attacked by Orlick she becomes a helpless object of pity and dies not long afterwards. Her funeral is ridiculous thanks to the greed of the local undertakers.

MOLLY

CHECKPOINT 42 **A01**

The nervous movements of Molly's fingers at Jaggers's dinner party (p. 381) is compared to what activity?

We first meet Molly, Estella's birth mother, as Jaggers's housekeeper – a significant moment in Chapter 48. Her manner is nervous and intense. Pip realises Molly is Estella's biological mother, saying he compared her 'with other hands, other eyes, other hair, that I knew of' (Ch. 48, p. 382). Wemmick says she is a 'wild beast tamed' (Ch. 38, p. 383) and tells Pip how she came to know Jaggers when he was her lawyer who helped her to avoid a guilty verdict in a murder trial (although Jaggers came to suspect she had been guilty after all).

COMPEYSON

A man of privileged background, Compeyson falls into crime out of greed, involving Magwitch. When they are both caught Compeyson uses his upper-class connections to save himself from transportation, causing Magwitch great frustration and resentment. Compeyson gets involved with Miss Havisham's half-brother, leading him to get engaged to her but deliberately leaving her before the wedding. It is said that she 'perfectly idolised him' (Ch. 22, p. 176). Compeyson tries to have Magwitch re-arrested in London but dies when Magwitch pushes him into the river Thames, with a 'white terror' (Ch. 54, p. 436) on his face.

PROGRESS AND REVISION CHECK

SECTION ONE: CHECK YOUR KNOWLEDGE

1 Who nicknames Pip 'Handel' after a piece of music about a blacksmith (Ch. 22, p. 173)?

2 Who terrifies Pip with a stick called the 'Tickler' (Ch. 2, p. 7)?

3 What does Miss Havisham say is the only reason for the Pockets coming to visit Satis House?

4 Who calls his father an 'aged parent' (Ch. 25, p. 199)?

5 Who does Joe Gargery marry?

6 Who is described as eating like a 'dog' (Ch. 3, p. 17)?

7 Who are Flopson and Millers?

8 Who has 'two ghastly casts' (Ch. 36, p. 280) on his office wall?

9 Where does Magwitch die?

10 Who says 'Here's Miss Skiffins! Let's have a wedding' (Ch. 55, p. 444)?

TOP TIP (A01)

Answer these quick questions to test your basic knowledge of the novel's characters.

SECTION TWO: CHECK YOUR UNDERSTANDING

Task: In Chapter 25, how does Dickens present the family relationship between Wemmick and his father?

Think about:

- how Dickens uses humour and imagery to bring the characters of Wemmick and his father to life
- how their relationship compares with other relationships in the book

TOP TIP (A01)

This task requires more thought and a slightly longer response. Try to write at least three to four paragraphs.

PROGRESS CHECK

GOOD PROGRESS

I can:

- Explain the significance of the main characters in how the action develops. ☐
- Refer to how they are described by Dickens and how this affects the way we see them. ☐

EXCELLENT PROGRESS

I can:

- Analyse in detail how Dickens has shaped and developed characters over the course of the novel. ☐
- Infer key ideas, themes and issues from the ways that characters and relationships are presented by Dickens. ☐

THEMES

THEME TRACKER (A01)

Self-knowledge

- Ch. 14, p. 104: Pip reflects on the importance of Joe in his life.
- Ch. 17, p. 124: Biddy points out Pip's selfishness, although Pip ignores her opinion.
- Ch. 56, p. 451: Pip acknowledges his love for Magwitch.

KEY CONTEXT (A03)

The Victorians were fascinated by the **Bildungsroman**, a novel that explore one person's journey through life and the moral decisions they have to make. Another example is Charlotte Brontë's *Jane Eyre* (1847).

SELF-KNOWLEDGE

Self-knowledge or self-discovery is a typical theme in this kind of Victorian **novel** that follows one person closely through the main events of their life:

- Pip rejects his working-class origins at the forge and aspires to become a gentleman. Even when he is apprenticed to Joe, he realises his time spent at the aristocratic Satis House has changed his opinions, saying he 'had a strong conviction on me that I should never like Joe's trade' (Ch. 13, p. 103).
- Pip is given wealth and is taught table manners and how to speak in a different way, but he loses his kindness and humanity in the process.

It is only through hardship, loss and the example of Joe Gargery's kindness in particular, that Pip comes to realise the emptiness of his ambitions. Joe Gargery, in contrast, is an example of a **character** who does not change:

- Throughout the novel Joe tells Pip, 'What larks!' (Ch. 57, p. 462) and 'Ever the best of friends!' (Ch. 57, p. 459) to demonstrate their friendship, however unpleasant Pip may be.
- Pip realises that Joe is content at the forge and never loses his basic decency and honesty. Pip reflects on this in Chapter 14, p. 104.

Estella goes on a journey of self-knowledge, and although she is aware of what she is doing she makes the mistake of thinking that she cannot be hurt by such a destructive way of life:

- Estella's experiences with Drummle and the passing of time make her realise what she has lost by rejecting Pip's love. At the end of the novel she remarks, possibly in reference to how she has aged, 'I am greatly changed!' (Ch. 59, p. 474).
- Pip notices that her touch is now 'friendly' when once it was 'insensible' (Ch. 59, p. 474).

AIMING HIGH: WRITING ABOUT A MINOR CHARACTER

A question about self-knowledge or self-discovery might suggest that the answer should be about Pip. However, you could tackle a less obvious character and so demonstrate detailed knowledge of the subtle features of the text. Miss Havisham is another character who goes on a journey of self-discovery. However, unlike Pip, for decades she has declined to improve her situation as she sits in her decaying wedding dress in Satis House. **Symbolically**, she 'afterwards stopped all the clocks' (Ch. 22, p. 176) and 'secluded herself from a thousand natural and healing influences' (Ch. 49, p. 390). When she realises the devastation she has brought to Estella's life she is overwhelmed by the sudden self-knowledge that all this has been 'vanity' (Ch. 49, p. 390): Dickens repeats the phrases 'vanity of remorse, the vanity of unworthiness' to show Miss Havisham's mental anguish. She cries 'What have I done!' (Ch. 49, p. 389): an unanswerable **rhetorical** question.

JUSTICE

There are two kinds of justice in *Great Expectations*: the justice of the law courts and the justice of the way we punish or reward ourselves and each other for our behaviour, called 'natural justice'. In terms of natural justice, loyalty and goodness are rewarded in the novel. Dickens was very keen to write about moral behaviour and to explore what is right or wrong:

- Pip comments on the 'injustice' of his treatment when a child by Mrs Joe (Ch. 8, p. 60).
- We feel that true and faithful Herbert deserves his happy marriage to Clara and that Joe and Biddy deserve their happiness together. Pip looks to Joe and Biddy for examples of good behaviour and asks, 'pray tell me, both, that you forgive me!' (Ch. 58, p. 470).
- We may also hope that Pip and Estella are allowed a happy future after they have both paid for their selfish and thoughtless behaviour.
- Magwitch tries to reward Pip for helping him on the marshes, saying 'I'm making a better gentleman nor ever *you*'ll be!' (Ch. 39, p. 315).
- Compeyson pays the ultimate price for his past crimes, which the legal system had failed to do.

The legal justice system itself is shown to be violent, unfair and open to manipulation by the likes of Jaggers:

- Jaggers has tried to counter the effects of this system by having Estella, the daughter of two violent criminals, adopted: 'one pretty little child out of the heap that could be saved' (Ch. 51, p. 404).
- Jaggers is surrounded by wretched clients who are desperate for his help to evade punishment for crimes they have committed (Ch. 20, p. 161).

KEY QUOTATION: MAGWITCH'S TRIAL (A02)

When Magwitch is put on trial for returning to England from Australia it is clear he is guilty by his very presence. Dickens presents a shocking **image** of the cruelty of the Victorian court system as thirty-two people, including Magwitch, are sentenced to death, demonstrating that their lives are not even worth an individual trial. Dickens describes the scene: 'The sheriffs with their great chains and nosegays, other civic gewgaws and monsters, criers, ushers, a great gallery full of people – a large theatrical audience – looked on, as the two-and-thirty and the Judge were solemnly confronted' (Ch. 56, p. 448). The details of the 'great chains' that symbolise power and the 'nosegays' that protected the sheriffs from the stink of the prisoners reinforce the inhumanity of the scene; the adjective 'theatrical' suggests that this is a form of entertainment to the observers.

Wealth and power

- Ch. 11, p. 83: Miss Havisham's wealth and power cause the Pockets to behave in a silly and irrational way.
- Ch. 34, p. 268: Pip and Herbert fall into debt.
- Ch. 58, p. 471: Pip and Herbert eventually pay off their debts and get good jobs.

WEALTH AND POWER

In *Great Expectations*, wealth, power and high social position may bring people misery:

- Miss Havisham's wealth brings her no comfort at all: she is brought up as a 'spoilt child' whose 'father denied her nothing' (Ch. 22, p. 174). Compeyson conspired against her with her half-brother to take the proceeds from the sale of the brewery.
- She uses her wealth as a tool to upset her grasping relatives and, through Estella, to get her revenge on the male sex.
- Bentley Drummle has wealth but is a brutal and ignorant bully whose aristocratic background gives him the freedom to behave in this way, his nature being 'nursed' by his family (Ch. 25, p. 197).
- Jaggers has great power in the legal world but is unmarried and feared by those around him.

It is the human values of love and kindness, as demonstrated by Herbert, Clara, Wemmick and Joe, that bring happiness in the **novel**:

- Wemmick may talk about the importance of 'portable property' (Ch. 24, p. 196) but his greatest happiness lies in warm human relationships and his simple pleasures in Walworth.

EXAM FOCUS: THE IMPORTANCE OF MONEY (A02)

This candidate is describing how Pip learns about the role and importance of money:

> Pip learns to be grateful for Joe, not because Joe has any money, but because Joe had so abundantly given the wealth of his great nature' (Ch. 57, p. 458). This quote uses the abstract noun 'wealth' in a metaphorical way to mean the riches that come from Joe's great kindness rather than wealth in terms of money. This shows how Pip has learnt to distinguish between the two as part of his journey towards maturity in the novel. Furthermore, near the end of the novel, Pip reflects with pleasure on his business with Herbert as one that did not make 'mints of money' but more importantly that they 'had a good name, and worked for our profits' (Ch. 58, p. 471) which again demonstrates that Pip has developed values that do not depend on financial wealth.

Correct technical terminology to explain the effect of Dickens's language

Connective develops the line of thought

Selects helpful quotations from across the text

Now you try it:

Give another example of how Pip learns about the role and importance of money. Start: *Another way that Pip learns about the value of money is through…*

PRIDE AND REVENGE

Pride and the desire for revenge are shown to be extremely destructive:

- Miss Havisham feeds these destructive forces by keeping around her the reminders of her humiliation and betrayal. Her life is distorted. She lives in the dark and ruins the lives of Estella and Pip through her obsession.
- Herbert refers to Miss Havisham's upbringing: 'Mr Havisham was very rich and very proud. So was his daughter' (Ch. 22, p. 174).
- Miss Havisham's devastation at being deserted by Compeyson is tied up in part with her personal pride, and leads to the 'wild resentment' that takes over her life (Ch. 49, p. 390).
- Orlick harbours resentment and vows to take revenge for what he sees as injustices.
- He attacks Mrs Joe in revenge for Pip being made an apprentice, and admits this in Ch. 53, p. 419.
- His pride is hurt because he sees Pip being given a lifetime trade.
- Orlick conspires with Compeyson and eventually attempts to murder Pip, saying 'You was always in Old Orlick's way ever since you was a child' (Ch. 53, p. 416).
- Magwitch is driven by pride and the need for revenge on Compeyson who has used his wealthy background to evade punishment by the courts.
- Readers may find Magwitch's desire for revenge more understandable, even though it leads him to desperate acts.

KEY QUOTATION: MAGWITCH'S NEED FOR REVENGE (A02)

In Chapter 5, the guards are searching for the escaped convicts on the marshes with Joe and Pip following. They are astonished to find the two convicts fighting in a ditch rather than hiding or running away. This is because Magwitch decides it is more important to ensure that Compeyson is captured. When the sergeant points out that they are both going to be handcuffed and their fighting has not helped them, Magwitch replies, 'I don't expect it to do me any good. ... I took him. He knows it. That's enough for me' (Ch. 5, p. 34). Being responsible for Compeyson's recapture after his escape is more important to Magwitch's personal pride than his own freedom.

THEME TRACKER (A01)

Pride and revenge

- Ch. 5, p. 34: Magwitch's desire for revenge over Compeyson is first described.
- Ch. 49, p. 390: Pip reflects on Miss Havisham's devastating obsession with revenge on all men.
- Ch. 54, p. 435: Magwitch finally has his revenge on Compeyson as he pushes him into the Thames to drown.

KEY CONTEXT (A03)

It is helpful to remember that 'pride' here is being used in the negative sense, in that it was believed to be a sin to have too much regard for yourself over other people.

CHECKPOINT 43 (A02)

How does Trabb's boy dent Pip's pride in his new clothes?

CONTEXTS

INDUSTRIAL REVOLUTION

Charles Dickens was born in 1812 at a time of great change. The population still lived mainly in the countryside, but the Industrial Revolution, under way since about 1760, led to the rapid growth of cities. This is reflected in *Great Expectations* where Dickens contrasts life in the Kent marshes with the busy city life in London. The growth of cities and industrialised factory methods was so rapid that the housing available to the poor was often appalling – as hinted in the details about Magwitch's life, for example.

KEY QUOTATION: THE CHANGING VICTORIAN LANDSCAPE (A01)

When Pip visits Satis House after the death of Miss Havisham, he 'saw the auctioneer's clerk walking on the casks and telling them off for the information of a catalogue-compiler, pen in hand' (Ch. 58, p. 465). The fall of Satis House could be seen here as a reflection of the changing social landscape of Britain in the mid-nineteenth century.

FEAR OF REVOLUTION

After the French Revolution in 1789 the British government feared revolution at home and sought to prevent challenge and protest: people could be imprisoned without trial and public executions and transportation to the colonies were common. The power of the legal system is reflected in the figure of Jaggers and the harsh treatment of Magwitch.

DICKENS AS A SOCIAL REFORMER

Dickens used his fame to publicise inequality in society. In *Great Expectations* the privileged Compeyson escapes transportation whereas the poor and virtually illiterate Magwitch is sent away: most of those transported were poor, uneducated people accused of theft. Dickens describes the use of manacles and leg-irons, the existence of the unsafe and overcrowded 'hulks', the frequent use of the death penalty even for minor crimes and the unfair way that the poor struggled to afford legal representation, making lawyers like Jaggers particularly powerful.

Great Expectations reflects Dickens's interests in children, their need for access to schooling and literacy, and domestic violence, following his own unhappy childhood. There are some corrupt schools and neglectful teachers in his novels, but the kind-hearted school mistress Biddy is a quiet heroine: the description of Joe writing (Ch. 57, p. 455) reflects her achievements. The fear that Pip feels at the hands of the violent and abusive Mrs Joe, the miserable childhoods of Joe Gargery and Magwitch, even the chaotic Pocket household overrun with children and nurses are typical of Dickens's explorations of how Victorian children were treated, and mistreated.

AIMING HIGH: WRITING ABOUT DICKENS'S LIFE ⭐

Remember that you will only be awarded marks when you link any knowledge you have about Dickens's life to your understanding of the novel. A successful answer may contain a comment such as this:

There is a common theme in 'Great Expectations' of troubled childhoods and this may stem from the fact that Dickens himself had a difficult relationship with his own parents throughout his life. Pip, Joe, Estella and Magwitch all have parents that are either abusive or neglectful. For example, Joe describes the way that he and his siblings were taken out of school and 'hammered' (Ch. 7, p. 44) by his father, with Dickens using a shocking word 'hammered' to convey the violence Joe suffered.

Aim always to link your comments to a specific detail from the novel and learn relevant quotations that you can use to provide evidence of your ability to write about Dickens's use of language.

KEY CONTEXT (A03)

Dickens's own experience of poverty and the legal system shaped much of his writing. In his novel *Little Dorrit* (1857) he describes a debtors' prison, in which his own father was locked up at one point.

SETTINGS

THE FORGE

The novel opens near Pip's home at the forge on the Kent marshes. The setting is bleak and described as a 'dark flat wilderness' (Ch. 1, p. 1). Pip is in the cemetery that contains the burial place of his siblings and parents, and although this may seem tragic to modern readers, such numbers of dead in one family were not unusual to Victorian readers. The setting contains a 'gibbet' (Ch. 1, p. 5), a reminder of death and punishment. The forge is not a place that Pip is fond of, and it is here that he has his final meeting with the murderous Orlick, under a 'red large moon' (Ch. 53, p. 412), **symbolising** danger.

LONDON

Dickens lived much of his life in London and uses his knowledge of it to symbolise Pip's aims and 'great expectations' which ultimately come to ruin and devastation. It is significant that the first part of London that Pip encounters is Smithfield market, 'all asmear with filth and fat and blood and foam' (Ch. 20, p. 160), contradicting Pip's romantic dreams. Walworth, in contrast, is a family home in which Wemmick lives happily with his father, reminding us that it is possible to have a happy and harmonious life.

REVISION FOCUS: LINKING SETTING TO THEME

Dickens uses setting carefully in order to develop the novel as a whole. For example, the ruined and menacing Satis House represents the themes of decay and descent into madness. There is a sense of **pathetic fallacy** in the reactions of the cattle on the marshes in Chapter 3: they seem to be aware of the young Pip's theft of the food from the pantry and watch him in an 'accusatory manner' (p. 14). Make a list of key settings and the themes they are linked to.

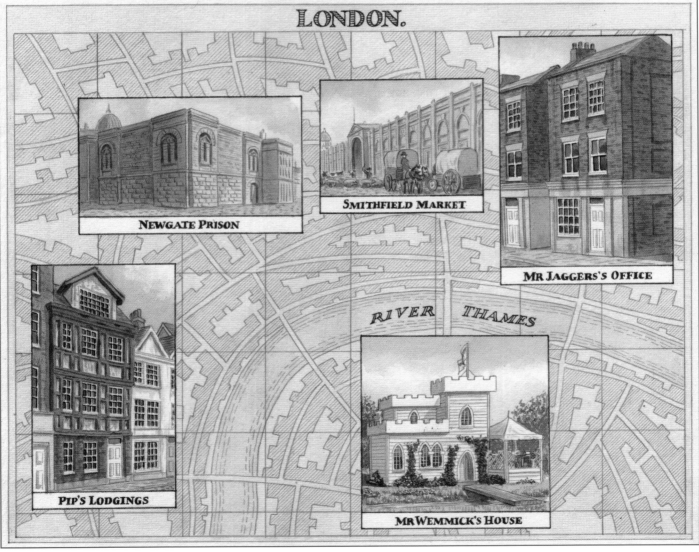

PROGRESS AND REVISION CHECK

SECTION ONE: CHECK YOUR KNOWLEDGE

1 What punishment does Magwitch face for returning to England from Australia, which Pip believes is unjust?

2 Who left Miss Havisham on the day of her wedding, leading to her desire for revenge on all men?

3 What business was once run at Satis House but falls into disrepair, leaving barrels and storerooms as part of the setting?

4 Whose office can be found in 'Little Britain' near the terrifying Smithfield meat market?

5 In which country had there been a revolution in 1789, leading to many people like Dickens questioning the social order in Britain?

6 Who dies regretting her vanity and selfishness in her final moments?

7 As part of the theme of justice and crime, what does Pip steal from the pantry to give to Magwitch?

8 What crime is Molly accused of?

9 What job is Pip apprenticed to as a young boy?

10 How does Magwitch finally get his revenge on Compeyson?

> **TOP TIP** (A01)
>
> Answer these quick questions to test your basic knowledge of the themes, contexts and settings of the novel.

SECTION TWO: CHECK YOUR UNDERSTANDING

Task: In Chapter 36, how does Dickens present the theme of money and business?

Think about:

- how Jaggers and Wemmick discuss money
- Pip and Herbert getting into difficulties with money and debt

> **TOP TIP** (A01)
>
> This task requires more thought and a slightly longer response. Try to write at least three to four paragraphs.

PROGRESS CHECK

GOOD PROGRESS

I can:

- Explain the main themes, contexts and settings in the novel and how they contribute to the effect on the reader.   ☐
- Use a range of appropriate evidence to support any points I make about these elements.   ☐

EXCELLENT PROGRESS

I can:

- Analyse in detail the way themes are developed and presented across the novel.   ☐
- Refer closely to key aspects of context and setting and the implications they have for the writer's viewpoint, and the interpretation of relationships and ideas.   ☐

FORM

OVERVIEW

The novel *Great Expectations* takes different forms, varying according to the stage in Pip's life: it is largely a Bildungsroman with Gothic features.

BILDUNGSROMAN

A Bildungsroman is a novel that tells the story of one person growing up and becoming an adult. It is a common form, and Dickens wrote more than one Bildungsroman: his others include *Oliver Twist* (1838) and *David Copperfield* (1850). A modern Bildungsroman is J. K. Rowling's *Harry Potter* series (1997–2007). A Bildungsroman has distinct features:

- There is a **sensitive main** character who searches for answers to life's problems.
- The story may begin with an **emotional loss** or difficulty (both Pip and Harry Potter are orphans with sad childhoods).
- The main character sets out to **explore the world** and leaves his/her childhood world (Pip leaves for London).
- The **goal** of this character is to be a mature, knowledgeable adult (the older Pip at the end of the novel is very different from the young Pip).
- There is often **conflict** with the world (e.g. Pip and Magwitch/Pip and Drummle/Pip and his embarrassment with Joe).
- The main character often **helps others at the end** of the novel because of all he/she has learnt (Pip forgives Miss Havisham and Magwitch and helps Herbert to set up his business).

THE GOTHIC

Since the 1750s, the Gothic has been a popular fictional form. Famous Gothic novels include Mary Shelley's *Frankenstein* (1818) and Bram Stoker's *Dracula* (1897), but many writers incorporate aspects of Gothic fiction into their work. Dickens does this in *Great Expectations*. These features include:

- **Reminders of death and unusual deaths**: the tombs containing Pip's parents and siblings (Ch. 1, p. 1); Miss Havisham's death by fire (Ch. 49, p. 394); the death masks in Jaggers's office (Ch. 20, p. 159).
- **Madness**: Miss Havisham's mental decline and 'mania' (Ch. 49, p. 390); Mrs Joe's terrifying 'Ram-page' (Ch. 2, p. 7).
- **Distinctive architecture**: the dark and decaying Satis House (Ch. 8, p. 54); Wemmick's quirky house (Ch. 25, p. 201); Jaggers's gloomy office (Ch. 20, p. 159).
- **Disguises and secrets**: Estella's mysterious parentage; Magwitch's return.
- **Gloomy weather and landscape**: the bleak Kent marshes (Ch. 1, p. 5); the stormy weather that accompanies Magwitch's return (Ch. 39, p. 307).

STRUCTURE

OVERVIEW

The novel was finally printed in the three 'stages' that it is printed in today (as shown on pp. 157 and 318), but it was first published in weekly instalments. This means that *Great Expectations* does not have the structure of a conventional novel. Instead of moving towards a general climax the story has lots of mini-cliffhangers and different plotlines in order to ensure that the public would buy the next episode. Sometimes it is compared to the soap-operas on television today.

THE NOVEL'S ENDING

Charles Dickens was persuaded to change the ending of the novel. Originally there was to be no Chapter 59.

- The novel was to have ended with Estella remarrying after Drummle's death. There would have been a meeting between Pip and Estella some years later but no future for the two as a couple. This ending was preferred by Dickens as he felt that it was more realistic than a romantic one.

- Dickens changed his mind after visiting his friend and fellow novelist Sir Edward Bulwer-Lytton, who thought that the original ending was too disappointing. Dickens quickly wrote the ending that has subsequently been used in all editions, in which Pip suggests he cannot see himself parting from Estella.

AIMING HIGH: WRITING ABOUT NARRATIVE DEVICES

Commenting on structure is a difficult skill but is rewarded by examiners. Remember that Dickens has other devices to help us learn about times and events that Pip was not there to witness himself. This may be called exposition, which means filling in background gaps. Methods include having other characters speak at length to fill in the gaps in the story, for example Herbert Pocket tells Pip how Miss Havisham came to be so miserable (Chapter 22, 'Satis House Explained'). Dickens also wants the reader to be aware that Pip is telling us his story, and so he speaks directly to the reader, using phrases such as 'as I proceed to relate' (Ch. 17, p. 129) and 'I must give one chapter to Estella' (Ch. 37, p. 293).

CHECKPOINT 45 **A03**

What was Dickens's profession before he became a novelist, which trained him to write accurately and with detail?

TOP TIP **A01**

Remember that in writing about *Great Expectations* you must always back up your comments with actual details and quotations.

LANGUAGE

OVERVIEW

Dickens is famous for his use of language to describe people, places and features of landscape. He uses a wide vocabulary, imagery and symbolism. Dickens also uses non-standard spelling to convey the different ways that characters speak. There is a good deal of descriptive language as well as very specific language linked to jobs, people and places.

TOP TIP (A01)

Pip's language is standard English – he does not use slang or dialect words, for example, and he often uses complex Latin-based words such as 'expostulatory' (Ch. 18, p. 139) and 'perplexities' (Ch. 34, p. 268) which is typical of a well-educated Victorian gentleman.

LANGUAGE DEVICE: NARRATIVE VOICE

What is narrative voice?	The way in which the narrator of the story addresses the reader
Example	Pip is the only narrative voice in the novel because it is written entirely from his point of view, opening with the first-person pronoun 'My...' (Ch. 1, p. 1).
Effect	This helps us to empathise with Pip.

- Pip is writing as an adult looking back on his life. At times his narrative voice is quite detached as if he can see his own younger self from a distance, for example in the first chapter he refers to himself in the third person, 'the small bundle of shivers growing afraid if it all, and beginning to cry, was Pip' (Ch. 1, p. 2).

- Pip is telling the story from his memories, but he does not give away plot lines. For example, the adult Pip knew that Magwitch would turn out to be someone very dear to him by the end of the novel. However, his narration generally reflects his experience at the time, so the first description of Magwitch is 'A fearful man, all in coarse grey' (Ch. 1, p. 2). This helps to make the story more believable and to create suspense.

- Pip is honest about his own weaknesses, such as when he reflects on his poor treatment of Joe when he visits Pip in London, confessing 'I was lost in the mazes of my future fortunes, and could not retrace the by-paths we had trodden together' (Ch. 18, p. 138).

REVISION FOCUS: LANGUAGE OF 'BUSINESS'

In order to make the world of his characters as believable as possible, Dickens uses the appropriate language for their occupations. You could make lists of **legal language** used by Wemmick and Jaggers, **business language** used by Herbert and Pumblechook, and words associated with **crime and illegal activity** used by Magwitch, for example.

LANGUAGE DEVICE: SENTENCE STRUCTURE

What is sentence structure?	The length and organisation of sentences using clauses and phrases
Example	A simple sentence uses one main **verb**, such as 'His spirit *inspired* me with great respect' (Ch. 11, p. 89). Compound sentences use more than one verb either in a list or joined by **connectives**.
Effect	Simple sentences can have a powerful and direct effect, conveying a distinct thought or image.

- Dickens writes in a typical Victorian prose style using compound sentences and complex structure.

- For example, the verbs, punctuation and connectives in the following complex sentence help Dickens convey richness and variety of detail: 'On every rail and gate, wet *lay* clammy; and the marsh-mist *was* so thick, that the wooden finger on the post *directing* people to the village – a direction which they never *accepted*, for they never *came* there – *was* invisible to me until I *was* quite close under it' (Ch. 3, p. 14).

- Look for the verbs in a sentence and count them up: this will help you decide if it is a simple or complex sentence.

LANGUAGE DEVICE: USE OF IMAGERY

What is imagery?	The use of **metaphors**, **similes** and **personification** to describe a person, feeling or place
Example	Joe is described with a simile: 'I have often thought him since like the steam-hammer, that can crush a man or pat an egg-shell, in his combination of strength with gentleness' (Ch. 18, p. 138).
Effect	This shows clearly the two different sides to Joe: strength and gentleness.

- It is helpful to remember that although Dickens is writing prose, he frequently uses similes, metaphors and personification to describe things in *Great Expectations*.

- It is easy to recognise a simile because of the use of 'like' and 'as' to compare things. If a description cannot be literally true then it may well be a metaphor. For example, Pip advises Herbert to deal with his debt: 'Look the thing in the face' (Ch. 34, p. 270).

- Sometimes imagery is used for a poetic effect. For example, Mill Pond Bank, where Magwitch stays on his return to London, is described as a place 'where the wind from the river had room to turn itself around' (Ch. 46, p. 365), personifying the wind.

TOP TIP **A01**

You may find that some of the words used by Dickens have fallen out of use or are archaic, such as 'guinea' (Ch. 18, p.137), an English coin worth just over a pound, or 'box-place' (Ch. 28, p. 219), a seat on a horse-driven coach.

LANGUAGE DEVICE: CHARACTONYM

Why are charactonyms significant?	Dickens invented names to reflect something of the character themselves, rather than trying to pick 'realistic' names.
Example	The name 'Pip' is not a common name; it could mean 'seed'.
Effect	'Pip' has connotations of growth and vulnerability, which are suitable for the character.

- Dickens is both famous for and sometimes criticised for this very specific use of invented names.
- In *Great Expectations*, Dickens uses many charactonyms, such as Estella ('star', reflecting how the character casts a light on Pip's life); Jaggers (describing the solicitor's tough and prickly manner); Pumblechook (reflecting his ridiculous manner); and 'Biddy' (suggesting her biddable or amenable and friendly personality).
- Nicknames also have a role in characterisation, such as 'Spider' for Drummle which suggests his unpleasant nature.

LANGUAGE DEVICE: USE OF SPEECH

What is use of speech?	How Dickens represents the ways that different characters speak
Example	'I'm oncommon fond of reading, too … On-common. Give me … a good book, or a good newspaper, and sit me down afore a good fire, and I ask no better' (Ch. 7, p. 43).
Effect	Joe Gargery becomes endearing through his humorous manner of speech.

- Dickens uses a variety of language techniques to represent the way that characters speak. He shows volume (how loudly a person speaks) through italics, for example, '"… it *is* hard," said Mrs Coiler' (Ch. 23, p. 186).
- He represents accent through spelling. The technique of depicting speech **phonetically** may give a comic edge, for example, Magwitch's words: 'You young dog … what fat cheeks you ha' got. … Darn me if I couldn't eat 'em … and if I han't half a mind to 't!' (Ch. 1, p. 2).
- Look at the way that Jaggers speaks as though presenting a case in court even when he is simply engaged in conversation, for example, 'Now Pip … put this case. Put the case that a woman, under such circumstances as you have mentioned, held a child concealed …' (Ch. 51, p. 404).

KEY CONTEXT (A03)

Dickens was famous for reading extracts of his **novels** out loud in public performances. Giving a range of different voices to his characters helped to bring the story to life and was very entertaining.

PROGRESS AND REVISION CHECK

SECTION ONE: CHECK YOUR KNOWLEDGE

1 What do the names 'Pumblechook' and 'Jaggers' suggest about the characters?

2 Dickens often writes down the way that characters speak phonetically. What does this mean?

3 In what ways is Jaggers's office a Gothic setting?

4 Why do the chapters in *Great Expectations* often end on cliffhangers?

5 What is Jaggers's nickname for Bentley Drummle and what does Dickens suggest about Drummle by choosing it?

6 Who uses an 'anvil' (Ch. 14, p. 103)?

7 The ivy at Satis House is described as having 'sinewy old arms' (Ch. 29, p. 226). What kind of imagery is being used?

8 Whose charactonym suggests she is helpful and friendly?

9 Magwitch says 'Thankye' (Ch. 54, p. 427) rather than 'thank you'. What speech feature is this?

10 Who often speaks as if he is presenting a case in court?

> **TOP TIP** (A01)
>
> Answer these quick questions to test your basic knowledge of the form, structure and language of the novel.

SECTION TWO: CHECK YOUR UNDERSTANDING

Task: In Chapter 3, how do we learn about the feelings and character of the young Pip through the first-person narrative voice?

Think about:

- the way young Pip's guilty feelings influence his perceptions
- how Dickens uses language and imagery to describe Magwitch through Pip's eyes

> **TOP TIP** (A02)
>
> This task requires more thought and a slightly longer response. Try to write at least three to four paragraphs.

PROGRESS CHECK

GOOD PROGRESS

I can:

- Explain how the writer uses form, structure and language to develop the action, show relationships, and develop ideas. ☐
- Use relevant quotations to support the points I make, and refer to the effect of some language choices. ☐

EXCELLENT PROGRESS

I can:

- Analyse in detail Dickens's use of particular forms, structures and language techniques to convey ideas, create characters, and evoke mood or setting. ☐
- Select from a range of evidence, including apt quotations, to infer the effect of particular language choices, and to develop wider interpretations. ☐

PART SIX: PROGRESS BOOSTER

UNDERSTANDING THE QUESTION

For your exam, you will be answering an extract-based question and/or a question on the whole of *Great Expectations*. Check with your teacher to see what sort of question you are doing. Whatever the task, questions in exams will need **decoding**. This means highlighting and understanding the key words so that the answer you write is relevant.

BREAK DOWN THE QUESTION

Pick out the **key words** or phrases. For example:

Question: Read the following extract from Chapter 8, pp. 54–7 starting 'We went into the house through a side door …' to '… so like a shroud.'

How does Dickens present **dangerous or unpleasant settings in this extract** and in the **novel as a whole**?

What does this tell you?

- Focus on the **different environments and settings** in the novel.
- The word **'present'** tells you that you should focus on the ways that Dickens presents these settings.
- The phrases **'this extract'** and **'novel as a whole'** mean you need to start with the given extract and then widen your discussion to the rest of the novel, but sticking to the topic in both.

PLANNING YOUR ANSWER

It is vital that you generate ideas quickly, and plan your answer efficiently when you sit the exam. Stick to your plan and, with a watch at your side, tick off each part as you progress.

STAGE 1: GENERATE IDEAS QUICKLY

Very briefly **list your key ideas** based on the question you have **decoded**. For example:

- *Satis House seen from the point of view of Pip as a child*
- *Imagery of decay and death: Miss Havisham like a 'skeleton' juxtaposing life and death*
- *Other places that are threatening, e.g. Smithfield market, Jaggers's office, the sluice house on the marshes, prison*

STAGE 2: JOT DOWN USEFUL QUOTATIONS (OR KEY EVENTS)

- **From the extract**: 'No glimpse of daylight was to be seen ...'
- **From the novel as a whole**: 'the shameful place, being all asmear with filth and fat and blood and foam ...' (Ch. 20, p. 160)

STAGE 3: PLAN FOR PARAGRAPHS

Use paragraphs to plan your answer. For example:

Paragraph	Point
Paragraph 1:	**Introduce** the **argument** you wish to make. Various settings in *Great Expectations* play different roles in the novel and all represent different parts of Pip's life. Those that cause him the most distress and challenge are described as dangerous and threatening, e.g. Satis House and the Little Britain/ Newgate Prison area of London.
Paragraph 2:	**Develop** this argument. Include **details, examples** and other possible **points of view**. It could be about Satis House, the first place Pip visits outside of the forge: a mixture of wealth and decay; Miss Havisham's madness shown through its dark and rotten state; the **Gothic imagery** used.
Paragraph 3:	London, which poses a threat to Pip despite the fact he thought it would make his fortune. Highlight the detail at the market and outside the law courts.
Paragraph 4:	How Pip feels threatened as he tries to help Magwitch escape: 'I had a feeling we were caged and threatened' (Ch. 54, p. 433).
(You may want to add further paragraphs if you have time.)	
Conclusion:	**Sum up** your argument: setting is a vital part of the novel that helps the reader understand the emotions and problems faced by the **characters**.

TOP TIP (A02)

When discussing Dickens's language, make sure you refer to the techniques he uses and, most importantly, the **effect** of those techniques. Don't write: *Dickens uses lots of adjectives in Chapter 54 ...* Instead, write: *Dickens's use of adjectives 'hunted, wounded, shackled' in Chapter 54 conveys Magwitch's desperate life in just three words.*

RESPONDING TO WRITERS' EFFECTS

The two most important assessment objectives are **AO1** and **AO2**. They are about *what* writers do (the choices they make, and the effects these create), *what* your ideas are (your analysis and interpretation), and *how* you write about them (how well you explain your ideas).

ASSESSMENT OBJECTIVE 1

What does it say?	What does it mean?	Dos and Don'ts
Read, understand and respond to texts. Students should be able to: • Maintain a critical style and develop an informed personal response • Use textual references, including quotations, to support and illustrate interpretations	You must: • Use some of the literary terms you have learned (correctly!) • Write in a professional way (not a sloppy, chatty way) • Show you have thought for yourself • Back up your ideas with examples, including quotations	**Don't write:** *Miss Havisham is a bit weird. Dickens uses lots of different words to describe her, like 'wild'.* **Do write:** *Dickens presents Miss Havisham as a complex and frightening figure. When Pip meets her she is domineering and powerful: '"Call Estella," she repeated, flashing a look at me' (Ch. 8, p. 57). At the end of her life Dickens uses the adjectives 'wild' (Ch. 49, p. 390) and 'afraid' (Ch. 49, p. 387) to describe her.*

IMPROVING YOUR CRITICAL STYLE

Use a variety of words and phrases to show effects. For example:

Dickens *suggests …, conveys …, implies…, presents …, explores …*

I/we (as readers) *infer …, recognise …, understand …, question …*

For example, look at these two alternative paragraphs by different students about Jaggers. Note the difference in the quality of expression:

Student A:

This sounds as if Charles Dickens is speaking!

It could 'mean' this, but there are other possibilities

'Bothered about' could mean lots of things and is unhelpful

Dickens says that Jaggers is really mean to Molly at the dinner party in Chapter 48. Jaggers says, 'Molly, Molly, Molly, Molly, how slow you are today!' This means that Jaggers is cross with Molly and he is trying to show off in front of Pip, Drummle and the other guests. Dickens is saying Jaggers isn't bothered about Molly.

This language is too chatty and informal

It is better to use an alternative word or phrase, other than 'saying'

Student B:

The word 'presents' shows awareness of Dickens as a writer

This helps the student introduce an interpretation – he/ she is not saying 'this is what it means'

Dickens presents Jaggers in an unpleasant light in Chapter 48 in the way that he treats Molly the housekeeper. Dickens describes Jaggers as being 'sharp' with Molly – this suggests that Jaggers is rude to her. We are also shown Jaggers being more sensitive to Pip's feelings, as he 'went on with dinner' and does not reveal that Pip has guessed that Molly is Estella's mother. This implies that Jaggers has both a kind and a menacing side to him.

This is a helpful use of an embedded quote

ASSESSMENT OBJECTIVE 2

What does it say?	What does it mean?	Dos and Don'ts
Analyse the language, form and structure used by the writer to create meanings and effects, using relevant subject terminology where appropriate.	'Analyse' = comment **in detail** on **particular aspects** of the text or language. 'Language' = vocabulary, imagery, variety of sentences, dialogue/speech, etc. 'Form' = how the story is told (e.g. first person narrative, letters, diaries) 'Structure'= the order in which events are revealed, or in which characters appear 'Create meaning' = What can we, as readers, infer from what the writer tells us? What is implied by particular descriptions, or events? 'Subject terminology' = words you should use when writing about novels, such as character, protagonist, imagery, setting, etc.	**Don't write:** *The writing is really descriptive in this bit so I get a picture of the Marshes.* **Do write:** *Dickens conveys the sense that the setting of the forge on the Kent marshes reflects some of the hardships that the main narrator Pip has to face. It is a lonely and dangerous place and there is a Gothic element to the 'tombstones'.*

THE THREE 'I'S

- The best analysis focuses on specific ideas, events or uses of language and thinks about what is **implied**.

- This means looking beyond the obvious and beginning to draw **inferences**. On the surface, the marshes tell us that Pip lives a relatively poor life as an orphan with a sister who treats him cruelly. But what role does the setting of the marshes play in developing the story of Pip's 'great expectations' and his attitudes towards wealth and social class, for example?

- From the inferences you make across the text as a whole, you can arrive at your own **interpretation** – a sense of the bigger picture, a wider evaluation of a person, relationship or idea.

USING QUOTATIONS

One of the secrets of success in writing exam essays is to use quotations **effectively**. There are five basic principles:

1. Quote only what is most useful.
2. Do not use a quotation that repeats what you have just written.
3. Put quotation marks, e.g. ' ', around the quotation.
4. Write the quotation exactly as it appears in the original.
5. Use the quotation so that it fits neatly into your sentence.

EXAM FOCUS: USING QUOTATIONS

Quotations should be used to develop the line of thought in your essay and 'zoom in' on key details, such as language choices. The example below shows a clear and effective way of doing this:

> Dickens presents Mrs Joe – Pip's sister – as someone who is cruel and hard. He says that she has an apron ' fastened over her figure behind with two loops, ... a square impregnable bib in front, that was stuck full of pins and needles' (p. 6). This suggests that Mrs Joe is aggressive and doesn't let people get close to her.

Point

Quotation

Explanation/effect

However, really **high-level responses** will go further. They will make an even more precise point, support it with an even more appropriate quotation, focus in on particular words and phrases and explain the effect or what is implied to make a wider point or draw inferences. Here is an example:

> Dickens presents Mrs Joe as an abusive and volatile character who resents bringing Pip up after the death of their parents. Dickens uses the metaphor of the 'impregnable' apron full of 'pins and needles' (p. 6) to imply the way that Mrs Joe actively rejects any possibility of love and warmth around her in the forge. Pip, as narrator, comments that he saw 'no reason' why she wore the apron; through this Dickens is able to imply the unnecessary and pointless nature of Mrs Joe's bullying behaviour.

Precise point

Literary device

Focused quotations fluently embedded

Explanation/ implication/effect

Further development/link

SPELLING, PUNCTUATION AND GRAMMAR

SPELLING

Remember to spell correctly the **author's** name, the names of all the **characters**, and the **names of places**.

It is a good idea to list some of the key spellings you know you sometimes get wrong *before* the exam starts. Then use it to check as you go along. Sometimes it is easy to make small errors as you write but if you have your key word list nearby you can check it.

PUNCTUATION

Remember:

- Use **full-stops and commas in sentences accurately** to make clear points. Don't get caught between a long, rambling sentence that doesn't make sense, and a lot of short repetitive ones. Write in a fluent way, using linking words and phrases.

Don't write	Do write
Pip and Herbert are good friends they started off as enemies fighting at Satis House but they end up living together in London and Pip helps Herbert to learn how to live as a gentleman.	*Pip and Herbert become lifelong friends, despite their initial fight when they meet as boys at Satis House. As adults, they lodge together in London, where Herbert helps Pip learn about the skills and qualities of being a real 'gentleman'.*

GRAMMAR

When you are writing about the text, make sure you:

- Use the present tense for discussing what the writer does, e.g. Dickens **presents** Estella as a self-contained young woman.
- Use pronouns and references back to make your writing flow.

Don't write	Do write
While Joe seems to be a gentle and kind man, Joe's inability to stand up to Mrs Joe made him sometimes seem weak when he was talking to Mrs Joe.	*While Joe seems to be a gentle and kind man, **his** inability to stand up to Mrs Joe **makes** him sometimes **seem** weak while he is talking to **her**.*

TOP TIP

Unless you are studying OCR, spelling, punctuation and grammar (AO4) won't be formally assessed in your exam on *Great Expectations*. However, it is still important to ensure that you write accurately and clearly, in order to get your points across to the examiner in the best possible way.

TOP TIP

Practise your spellings of key literature terms you might use when writing about the text, such as ironic, simile, metaphor, imagery, protagonist, character.

TOP TIP A04

Enliven your essay by varying the way your sentences begin. For example, *'Pip is drawn to Estella, despite Estella's cold and remote manner'*, can also be written as *'Despite her cold and remote manner, Pip is drawn to Estella'*.

ANNOTATED SAMPLE ANSWERS

This section provides three sample responses, one at **mid** level, one at a **good** level and one at a **very high** level.

> **Question:** In Chapter 39, Magwitch returns to tell Pip he is his benefactor.
>
> Read from 'I could not have spoken one word …' (p. 313) to 'my blood ran cold within me' (p. 314).
>
> Starting with this extract, write about the ways that Dickens presents the relationship between Pip and Magwitch.
>
> Write about:
> - How Pip's feelings about Magwitch are described in the extract
> - How Dickens presents Pip's relationship with Magwitch as a whole

SAMPLE ANSWER 1

A01 Clear introduction to extract

This is a very important scene when Magwitch comes back to England to surprise Pip and to tell him that he has been his benefactor all along. Pip is very upset and horrified.

A01 Quotation could be more fluently embedded

Dickens describes Pip as saying 'I stood, with a hand on the chair-back'. Magwitch has to hold him up and then Magwitch kneels down and looks really closely at him. This reminds me of Chapter 1 when Pip meets Magwitch and Magwitch frightens him by holding him upside down and putting his face close to Pip's face which is scary for Pip. Pip says he is 'suffocating' too which also shows us how frightened he is. Magwitch is very scary in the beginning of the story so it is surprising to the reader that he becomes a kind person and gives Pip all his money.

A02 Personal response but could be more formally worded

A02 Puts the extract in the context of the novel

A01 More effective embedded quotation

Pip uses lots of words to show how much he dislikes Magwitch such as 'repugnance' and 'dread'. Pip says Magwitch is very ugly because he is a 'terrible beast'. Magwitch says he is not like a human because he is a 'dog'. This makes the fact that he made Pip into a gentleman much worse for Pip because Pip has spent all this time believing Miss Havisham wanted him to be a gentleman so he could marry Estella. This means that Magwitch is like a father to him and Magwitch says 'I'm your second father' although Pip has Joe Gargery who is also a kind of father to him. Magwitch says 'You're my son – more to me nor any son. I've put away money, only for you to spend.' Joe Gargery helps Pip a lot when Pip is little but when Pip is in London he thinks that Joe is embarrassing. Pip later learns that Joe is a kind of gentleman because of the kind way that he treats people.

A02
Too much about Joe – not relevant to question

A02
Attempts to analyse language feature but uses weak word 'rough'

Magwitch talks in rough language and uses words like 'wot' and 'ain't' whereas Pip always speaks politely in the book. This shows the difference between them. Pip tries to behave like a gentleman and can read and write but Magwitch never went to school and talks rough because he has been in prison and been a criminal for so long. Magwitch is described like a snake and Pip jumps when Magwitch touches him. When Magwitch kisses Pip's hand Pip says he is frightened because his blood ran 'cold'.

A01
Signals understanding of the plot

When Magwitch dies later in the book their relationship had got much better. Pip helped keep Magwitch safe from the police until they were caught on the river. Even Herbert had helped to keep Magwitch safe even though it was against the law. Pip uses a secret name for Magwitch called 'Provis' which helps to hide Magwitch but they get found out in the end. Pip tries to get Magwitch out of the prison. Dickens believed that the prison system was wrong in Victorian days and this is an example of how people were not treated fairly. Pip tells Magwitch that Estella is his daughter and that he loves her and that makes Magwitch die happy. This shows how their relationship has improved. Pip doesn't mind it when Magwitch holds his hand and calls him 'dear boy'.

A03
Some reference to the context of Dickens's attitudes towards the Victorian prison system

MID LEVEL

Comment
There are some good points and the answer looks at lots of different aspects of the extract and some parts of the book as a whole. There could be more references to Dickens as the writer and closer analysis of language, rather than giving straightforward explanations of what words mean without saying much about the effect of language.

For a Good Level:
- Try to use some relevant vocabulary to describe the language and Dickens's devices, such as imagery or non-standard English.
- Embed quotations rather than adding them on to statements.
- Try to keep sentences short or use connectives such as 'however' or 'although' or use semi-colons, to link ideas together.

SAMPLE ANSWER 2

A01 A basic introduction which sets up answer well

The relationship between Pip and Magwitch is very important to the novel and it links to the themes of parents and children as well as rich and poor. This extract tells us a lot about the relationship between Pip and Magwitch and is a dramatic plot twist.

A01 Quotation fluently embedded into the sentence

A02 Zooms in on key word and explains its effect

The news that Magwitch is Pip's benefactor makes Pip feel physically ill; he feels he is 'suffocating' and the room around him begins to 'surge and turn'. This ensures that the reader is clear that Pip had no idea that the source of his money would be Magwitch; in fact, Pip was led to believe that Miss Havisham had given him the money. Dickens says that he 'shuddered' as he looked closely into Magwitch's face, which has the effect of reminding the reader of the fear Pip felt for Magwitch as they first met in the churchyard.

A01 Paragraph introduces new point

Magwitch says he has 'made a gentleman' of Pip. The idea of being a 'gentleman' is central to Pip's life. Everything Pip has done in London has been to try to make himself a gentleman – this includes changing his clothes and learning gentlemanly behaviour from Herbert Pocket. Consequently, the fact that Magwitch – a violent and terrifying convict – has actually given Pip the means to be a 'gentleman' is a terrible shock. Dickens uses a rule of three when Pip describes his feelings as a mixture of 'abhorrence', 'dread' and 'repugnance', employing a rhetorical device that adds power and emphasis.

A02 Analysis of key word

A02 Literary device and its intended effect

A03 Comments on social context of the novel

Dickens's depiction of Magwitch's time in Australia is surprisingly moving; Dickens wrote this novel in part as a comment on the use of such inhumane punishments. Magwitch, for example, lives in a 'solitary' hut seeing no one else for many years. It almost seems that Magwitch has been driven mad with his obsession with Pip.

A01 Clear personal interpretation, well developed

This chapter shows the beginning of Pip's development into a more honest and kind man. It may be the lowest point of his fear and hatred of Magwitch, but as Pip comes to accept Magwitch as a father he also learns to appreciate the convict's genuine love and kindness. Knowing that Magwitch has risked his own life by coming to London to see him leads Pip to acknowledge his genuine devotion.

Although Magwitch is caught and sentenced to death for returning to Britain, Pip does all that he can to make Magwitch's final days good. In the extract Pip is upset by the way that Magwitch always calls him 'dear boy' but when Magwitch calls him 'dear boy' in the chapter called One Finds Peace (in which Magwitch dies) it feels more like a friendly term showing how their relationship develops. Pip spends many hours holding Magwitch's hand and is Magwitch's only visitor.

A01 Good reference showing plot development

The last thing that Pip says to Magwitch is to tell him about Estella. This is very kind of Pip and allows Magwitch to die happily. This also shows the structure of the novel in which relationships are generally resolved in some way. It also links to the way that Miss Havisham dies with Pip being able to say 'I forgive her' as she lays dead.

A02 Comment on structure and context

GOOD LEVEL

Comment

This is clearly written and explores some of the different aspects of the relationship between Pip and Magwitch across the novel. There is some close analysis of key words and phrases to get points across, and some evidence of personal interpretation. One language feature is noticed – the rule of three – but there could be one or two more such terms used, such as metaphor or imagery.

For a High Level:

- Develop the links to the rest of the novel, such as Miss Havisham, and the parallels between this extract and Chapter 1.
- Expand the style of expression by using a wider vocabulary so that more subtle ideas can be developed
- Quote more regularly from the extract.

SAMPLE ANSWER 3

A01

Excellent opening introduction sets up importance of extract in the action of the novel, and in the meeting between Pip and Magwitch

The relationship between Pip and Magwitch is a main feature of the entire novel. Through this relationship Dickens is able to explore many themes and ideas, such as the relationship between adults, parents and children, rich and poor, ambition and pride, and punishment and criminality. This extract could be considered as typically 'Dickensian' in that it contains not only a scene of gothic dread, but also elaborate linguistic features, dramatic plot revelation and, at its heart, great sentiment and high emotion.

A02

Excellent analysis of words and language techniques

Magwitch's disclosure of his identity has a devastating impact on Pip; Dickens portrays the physical effects of shock on Pip who 'grasped' at the chair, when the room began to 'surge and turn'. Verbs such as 'grasped' and 'suffocating' characterise Pip's panic and terror; the surging of the room recalls the way that Magwitch makes the world 'go head over heels' in the opening chapter of the novel when he picks up the young Pip in the cemetery. In both chapters Magwitch turns Pip's life upside down both physically and metaphorically. Dickens continues with the parallels between both scenes in describing how Magwitch 'caught' Pip and brought his face 'near to mine', and there is a shocking sense of Magwitch acting as a humble father as he bends on his knee in front of the helpless Pip and looks closely into his face.

A01

Useful reference back to earlier part of novel

A02

Clear, detailed analysis supported by well-selected quotation

Dickens employs powerful abstract nouns such as 'abhorrence', 'dread' and 'repugnance' in a tripartite rhetorical sequence in order to convey Pip's emotions. Pip's description of Magwitch as a 'terrible beast' again recalls the way the young Pip reacts to Magwitch in the opening chapter of the novel where Magwitch is portrayed as eating 'like a dog' and a 'madman'. Magwitch, in fact, described himself as a 'hunted dunghill dog' while a criminal out on the marshes, but the difference in this chapter is that the reformed Magwitch has dedicated his life to repaying Pip.

A further question is raised when Magwitch says 'I'm your second father. You're my son – more to me nor any son'. The notion is actually very problematic: it raises the question of who Pip's 'first' father is. In reality, that 'first father' died long before he could have any influence on Pip's life. Joe

A02 Excellent development of point, with interpretation of language and effect

Gargery is arguably a paternal influence, but Joe's relationship with Pip is blighted by Mrs Joe's humiliating and abusive behaviour, which emasculates Joe to the point where he is almost another child in the forge with Pip. Jaggers, Wemmick and Pumblechook all offer different kinds of paternal guidance but none of these fulfil the role of 'father' in the way that Magwitch, ironically, is able to do. It is, in fact, Magwitch's paternal love for Pip that motivates him to make so much money – as Magwitch says, 'In every single thing I went for, I went for you' (Ch. 39, p. 315).

A04 Well chosen vocabulary for literary device

Dickens juxtaposes Magwitch's euphoria, his 'heat and triumph', with Pip's physical and emotional shock, which results in Pip 'nearly fainting'. The contrast with reality is also emphasised by Magwitch's ideas of being a gentleman. To him it is a matter of wealth and acquisition – he offers money for 'wagers' with 'lords' and is exhilarated by the sight of Pip's 'linen', and his books 'mounting up, on their shelves, by hundreds'. The reader, of course, will be aware that these objects are ironically the cause of Pip's debt and are of no comfort to him at all. Moreover, Magwitch's physicality – he takes Pip's watch out of his pocket, and turns the ring on his finger – causes Pip to 'recoil' as if Magwitch were a 'snake' and Dickens's continuing use of animal symbolism conveys Pip's horror. When Magwitch kisses Pip's hands, Pip remarks that his blood 'ran cold' with Dickens here employing the gothic imagery of fear.

A02 Subtle analysis of Dickens's techniques using embedded quotes

A03 Comment on the genre of the Gothic in the novel

A01 Insightful link to other aspect of novel

However, this chapter ironically marks the beginning of Pip's development into a much more honest and compassionate man, because it is only by accepting Magwitch's fatherly love that he is able to come to terms with his own humble background. Furthermore, as part of the Bildungsroman structure, this scene portrays a conflict that the main protagonist has to overcome in order to progress and mature.

A01 Maintains critical style and uses critical term for novel structure with accuracy

VERY HIGH LEVEL

Comment
There is close focus on the scene and the question. The essay traces the development of the scene and its various connections to the other relationships, themes and ideas within the novel. It employs a clear, critical style and puts forward a range of interpretations showing full understanding.

PRACTICE TASK

Write a full-length response to this exam-style question and then use the **Mark scheme** on page 96 to assess your own response.

Question: In Chapter 27, Joe Gargery comes to visit Pip in London.

Read from 'As the time approached I should have liked to run away...' (p. 213) to '... the flowered pattern of my dressing gown' (p. 214).

How does Dickens present the relationship between Pip and Joe in the novel?

Write about:

- How Dickens presents Joe in this extract
- How he is presented in the rest of the novel

Remember:

- Plan quickly and efficiently by using key words from the question.
- Write equally about the extract and the rest of the novel.
- Focus on the techniques Dickens uses and their effect on the reader.
- Support your ideas with relevant evidence, including quotations.

FURTHER QUESTIONS

1 Read the extract in which Miss Havisham dies after a fire at Satis House.

It begins, 'Though every vestige of her dress was burnt ...' (Ch. 49, p. 394) and ends 'I forgive her' (Ch. 49, p. 395).

- Write about the ways that Dickens presents Miss Havisham.
- Refer to this extract and the story as a whole.

2 Read the extract in which Joe Gargery and Orlick have a fight after Orlick insults Mrs Joe.

It begins, 'Oh! To hear him!...' (Ch. 15, p. 111) and ends '... such is Life!' (Ch. 15, p. 112).

- Write about the ways that Dickens presents conflict in the story.
- Refer to this extract and the story as a whole.

3 'Pip is a selfish character throughout the novel.' How far do you agree with this view? Explore at least two moments from the novel to support your ideas.

4 Explore the ways that Dickens presents the theme of love in the novel.

- Consider the different types of love that exist in the book such as family love or married love, for example.
- Demonstrate how characters show their love for each other.

LITERARY TERMS

archaic	words that are no longer in everyday use
Bildungsroman	a novel that tells the story of one person's growth from childhood to maturity
character	a fictional person in a story
charactonym	a name given to a character which carries suggestions about that person's manner or appearance
cliffhanger	a device that ends a chapter in the middle of a dramatic event, leaving the reader wanting to read the next chapter
climax	the most important part of a narrative with the greatest emotional tension
connective	a word or phrase that joins clauses, sentences or paragraphs
device	a technique used by an author
dialect	regional forms of English that differ from 'standard English'
embody	being an example of a particular quality
empathise	to understand and share feelings experienced by others
farce	an improbable or laughable sequence of events
foreground	an important event or person is introduced in a significant way
Gothic	a style of writing that features elements of horror and the supernatural
hyperbole	writing in an exaggerated way for a particular effect, such as humour or shock
imagery	making pictures with words, using similes and/or metaphors
irony	saying or writing one thing when something else is meant
metaphor	a word or image which means one thing is used to represent another
narrative	a story told in a series of connected events
narrator	the voice telling the story
novel	a prose fiction with a central protagonist moving towards a climax and resolution; there may be many reversals
parody	to copy someone in a way that makes them look ridiculous or foolish
pathetic fallacy	giving objects and/or events in nature human emotions and traits
pathos	the depiction of events which evoke strong feelings of pity or sorrow
personification	giving an inanimate object or abstract concept human attributes or feelings
phonetically	writing words as they are spoken, not in conventional spelling
protagonist	the main character in a story, poem or play
rhetoric	language used to convey an argument or point of view
satire	a way of presenting a situation or person to show their unattractive behaviour
simile	a direct comparison; it will always contain a word such as 'like' or 'as'
standard English	the English that is used in formal speech and writing
style	how a writer says something
symbol	a sign that represents something else
tone	the way the narrator speaks to the reader or a character speaks to another
verb	a word that denotes an action

CHECKPOINT ANSWERS

PART TWO, pp. 8–49

1. To visit the graves of his parents and siblings. 2. Herbert Pocket. 3. The convict is later to reappear as Pip's benefactor. 4. Through the use of the brandy bottle with tar-water in it. 5. Mrs Joe puts up new curtains and makes polite conversation, instead of her normal cruel comments to Joe and Pip. 6. He is extremely frightened. 7. She is dressed as for her own wedding which should have taken place many years ago. 8. The bitterness of Miss Havisham seems to have affected her. 9. Estella has made Pip feel he is common; he decides to acquire an education. 10. So that we recognise him later. 11. Miss Havisham's relatives do not want to upset her in case she leaves them out of her will. 12. Miss Havisham is prepared to allow him to be humiliated as practice for Estella. 13. Pip is starting to feel that his simple life with the blacksmith is now beneath him. 14. Dickens is telling the reader that Orlick is sneaky and likes to make trouble. 15. Orlick becomes a thoroughly sinister character from this point onward. Dickens intends to use him again in the attack on Pip. 16. In reality this could only have been carried out by Orlick. 17. That Miss Havisham is preparing him to marry Estella. 18. Pip does not see that her behaviour points to her lack of interest in his future. 19. Even lawyers were prepared to cheat in order to win cases. 20. It brings some humour and light relief before the introduction of Drummle and the housekeeper in the next chapter. 21. Wemmick becomes warm and human when he goes home to Walworth. 22. Jaggers realises that Drummle is trouble. 23. He does not want to face the truth. 24. It is used as comic relief from the difficult subject of Estella which appears either side of it. 25. Jaggers knows Estella's parents, Molly and Magwitch. 26. In his desire to help Herbert in business. 27. We begin to see Miss Havisham as a pathetic figure as she begs for Estella's affection. 28. A storm precedes the arrival of Magwitch and its dramatic nature reflects the events of the story. 29. When Pip discovers the real identity of his benefactor, he is faced with his own vanity and gullibility; his life has been guided by fantasy. 30. Most of the blame for their crimes fell on Magwitch because Compeyson seemed such a gentleman. 31. As he leaves he has the impression that Miss Havisham regrets what she has done to Estella. 32. Dickens is telling us that the escape attempt will not go smoothly. 33. Pip gains dignity in his forgiveness of Miss Havisham. 34. Miss Havisham sees the harm that she has done and is filled with regret. 35. Orlick once considered marrying Biddy. 36. He has helped to establish Herbert as a partner in a business. 37. The British justice system could be cruel and uncaring.

PART THREE, pp. 52–62

38. He pretends he is Mrs Pumblechook's 'chaise-cart' (Ch. 8, p. 56) or carriage. 39. Pip imagines he sees Miss Havisham hanging in a building attached to Satis House (Ch. 8, p. 61). 40. The washing could suggest that Jaggers's job makes him feel uncomfortable or 'dirty' and he likes to 'wash' his clients away. 41. Pumblechook pretends to know what it is like in Satis House but by agreeing with Pip's made-up descriptions he shows his ignorance (Ch. 8, p. 53). 42. Knitting.

PART FOUR, pp. 64–70

43. Trabb's boy throws stones at Pip.

PART FIVE, pp. 72–6

44. It is called 'dialogue'. 45. Dickens was trained as a reporter in the law courts of London.

PROGRESS AND REVISION CHECK ANSWERS

PART TWO, pp. 50–1

SECTION ONE

1   Joe is a blacksmith.

2   Magwitch asks for 'wittles' or food.

3   The hulks were special ships that housed prisoners.

4   Estella lives with Miss Havisham.

5   Joe Gargery takes Pip as an apprentice blacksmith.

6   Leg-irons are found next to Mrs Joe, suggesting that an escaped convict may have attacked her (in fact, Orlick attacked her).

7   Pip first meets Herbert while visiting Miss Havisham at Satis House when they were both children.

8   Jaggers nicknames Bentley Drummle 'the Spider'.

9   Pip receives a five hundred pound note.

10   Magwitch calls himself Provis.

11   Pip mistakenly believes that Miss Havisham is his mysterious benefactor.

12   He sees the figure of Miss Havisham hanging from a beam in the gardens.

13   Jaggers arranged for the adoption of Estella by Miss Havisham.

14   Orlick ties Pip to a ladder and threatens to kill him.

15   He is sentenced to the death penalty.

16   Pip.

17   Mr Pumblechook.

18   Joe and Biddy call their son 'Pip'.

19   He is killed after being kicked by a horse he mistreated.

20   Pip becomes a partner in a firm with Herbert Pocket.

SECTION TWO

Task 1: Possible plan

- Pip can see the 'shameful' meat markets, the 'bulging' St Paul's and the 'grim' Newgate Prison, all of which **symbolise** power and fear (Ch. 20, p. 160).

- Jaggers's chair is compared to a 'coffin' and his office contains moulds of executed prisoners – it is alarming and intimidating (Ch. 20, p. 159).

- The office is surrounded by 'terrified', 'not by any means sober', 'dirty' and 'excitable' people desperate for Jaggers's attention which shows his power and importance (Ch. 20, pp. 160–4).

- Pip labels London as 'sickening' (Ch. 20, p. 160.

Task 2: Possible plan

- Orlick's physical strength contrasts with Pip's gentleness: for example, Orlick is described as 'a strong man's hand' (Ch. 53, p. 414).

- Pip was right to sense Orlick as a threat: 'I was in a dangerous strait indeed' (Ch. 53, p. 415).

- Orlick blames Pip and Mrs Joe for all of his failures: 'You and her *have* pretty well hunted me out of this country' (Ch. 53, p. 418).

- Dickens uses language and **imagery** to describe Orlick's threatening manner, such as 'tiger crouching to spring' (Ch. 53, p. 418).

PART THREE, p. 63

SECTION ONE

1 Herbert Pocket.

2 Mrs Joe.

3 To inherit money from her when she dies.

4 Wemmick.

5 Biddy.

6 Magwitch.

7 The Pockets' nursemaids.

8 Jaggers.

9 In Newgate Prison.

10 Wemmick.

SECTION TWO

Possible plan:

● The eccentric features of the house (fortifications and so on) are partly built by Wemmick to please his father.

● 'The Aged' is described as 'clean, cheerful, comfortable and well cared for' (Ch. 25, p. 202) contrasting with the violent Mrs Joe, Pip's adoptive mother; the relationship between Miss Havisham and Estella is highly destructive.

● Wemmick's face is described as 'softened' as he looks at his father (Ch. 25, p. 202).

● Dickens creates humour from the way that Pip nods repeatedly at 'the Aged' as a form of communicating, at one point nodding so much that 'I absolutely could not see him' (Ch. 25, p. 203).

PART FOUR, p. 71

SECTION ONE

1 Capital punishment by hanging.

2 Compeyson was engaged to marry Miss Havisham, but left her deliberately on the day of the wedding as part of his conspiracy with Miss Havishman's half-brother.

3 Satis House was a brewery.

4 Jaggers's office.

5 The 1789 French Revolution completely changed the social and political system in France.

6 Miss Havisham.

7 Food and brandy.

8 Murder.

9 Blacksmith.

10 By drowning him in the river Thames.

SECTION TWO

Possible plan:

● Jaggers correctly guesses that Pip is in debt; he clearly has a strong opinion that handing Pip the huge amount of money from his benefactor is 'injudicious' (Ch. 36, p. 282).

● Jaggers does not offer advice because he is 'not paid' to do so (Ch. 36, p. 282) – this could be interpreted as Dickens showing the greediness of lawyers who will do nothing unless they are being paid.

● Wemmick offers advice, edged with humour: he suggests that Pip should throw his money off a bridge rather than 'serve a friend' with it (Ch. 36, p. 285).

● Both Pip and Herbert are immature and fall into debt, but both have learnt to work hard and spend sensibly by the end of the novel.

PART FIVE, pp. 77

SECTION ONE

1 'Pumblechook' suggests his bumbling, ignorant manner; 'Jaggers' suggests his sharp and jagged personality.

2 Phonetic writing represents the way words are said through spelling, such as the way Joe says 'continiwally' when he means 'continually' (Ch. 27, p. 215).

3 It contains several references to death, such as death masks and a chair like a coffin.

4 The novel was published in a weekly periodical, which was like a magazine, and the cliffhangers encouraged readers to buy the next edition.

5 Jaggers calls Drummle 'the Spider', suggesting Drummle's threatening and repellent manner.

6 A blacksmith.

7 Personification.

8 Biddy.

9 Accent.

10 Jaggers.

SECTION TWO

Possible plan:

- Close attention to detail reflects Pip's misery and creates **pathetic fallacy**: for example, the 'clammy' air and the fog make everything seem to be a threat to Pip (Ch. 3, p. 14).
- Use of **Gothic imagery** – spiders' webs and the signpost that points Pip to the hulks like a 'phantom' – adds to the atmosphere (Ch. 3, p. 14).
- Dickens emphasises Pip's sympathy for Magwitch by the way Pip notices the physical details of the convict's misery: Magwitch is 'hugging and limping', for example, and he shivers 'violently' (Ch. 3, pp. 15–16).
- The disturbing image of Magwitch's throat clicking as if he is mechanical or his eating like a 'dog' (Ch. 3, p. 17) suggest he is less than human at times: these details are terrifying to the young Pip.

MARK SCHEME

POINTS YOU COULD HAVE MADE

- Pip's desire to 'run away' shows that he senses Joe is going to find this situation difficult.
- Dickens provides specific details about Joe's arrival – he is 'clumsy' and he has to trace Pip's name with his fingers.
- Pip is snobbish and has no sympathy for Joe.
- Joe's awkward way of copying Pip's speech and shaking his hand shows he is trying to behave suitably.
- Dickens's presentation of Joe's non-standard speech, e.g. 'growed', contrasts with Pip's careful standard English.
- Dickens uses humour in describing Joe's handling of his hat to show that Joe does not know the right 'rules' or etiquette (that Pip himself had to learn once from Herbert).
- From the opening of the novel, Joe has an ill-defined relationship with Pip that is neither really parent nor brother-in-law but all the same is loving and kind.
- Pip does not really appreciate Joe's qualities until later in the novel: it is Joe that nurses Pip back to health and clears Pip's debts.
- Overall, Dickens encourages us to see that Joe may be poor but he has gentlemanly qualities that Pip sometimes lacks.

GENERAL SKILLS

Make a judgement about your level based on the points you made (above) and the skills you showed.

Level	Key elements	Writing skills	Tick your level
Very High	**Very well-structured answer which gives a rounded and convincing viewpoint.** You use very detailed analysis of the writer's methods and effects on the reader, using precise references which are fluently woven into what you say. You draw inferences, consider more than one perspective or angle, including the context where relevant, and make interpretations about the text as a whole.	You spell and punctuate with consistent accuracy, and use a very wide range of vocabulary and sentence structures to achieve effective control of meaning.	
Good to High	**A thoughtful, detailed response with well-chosen references.** At the top end, you address all aspects of the task in a clearly expressed way, and examine key aspects in detail. You are beginning to consider implications, explore alternative interpretations or ideas; at the top end, you do this fairly regularly and with some confidence.	You spell and punctuate with considerable accuracy, and use a considerable range of vocabulary and sentence structures to achieve general control of meaning.	
Mid	**A consistent response with clear understanding of the main ideas shown.** You use a range of references to support your ideas and your viewpoint is logical and easy to follow. Some evidence of commenting on the writer's effects, though more needed.	You spell and punctuate with reasonable accuracy, and use a reasonable range of vocabulary and sentence structures.	
Lower	**Some relevant ideas but an inconsistent and rather simple response in places.** You show you have understood the task and you make some points to support what you say, but the evidence is not always well chosen. Your analysis is a bit basic and you do not comment in much detail on the writer's methods.	Your spelling and punctuation is inconsistent and your vocabulary and sentence structures are both limited. Some of these make your meaning unclear.	